Scorpio

Personality and Soul Characteristics Plus Rising Signs

(The Ultimate Guide to an Amazing Zodiac Sign in Astrology)

David Cannon

Published By **Chris David**

David Cannon

All Rights Reserved

Scorpio: Personality and Soul Characteristics Plus Rising Signs (The Ultimate Guide to an Amazing Zodiac Sign in Astrology)

ISBN 978-1-77485-530-0

No part of this guidebook shall be reproduced in any form without permission in writing from the publisher except in the case of brief quotations embodied in critical articles or reviews.

Legal & Disclaimer

The information contained in this ebook is not designed to replace or take the place of any form of medicine or professional medical advice. The information in this ebook has been provided for educational & entertainment purposes only.

The information contained in this book has been compiled from sources deemed reliable, and it is accurate to the best of the Author's knowledge; however, the Author cannot guarantee its accuracy and validity and cannot be held liable for any errors or omissions. Changes are periodically made to this book. You must consult your doctor or get professional medical advice before using any of the suggested remedies, techniques, or information in this book.

Upon using the information contained in this book, you agree to hold harmless the Author from and against any damages, costs, and expenses, including any legal fees potentially resulting from the application of any of the information provided by this guide. This disclaimer applies to any damages or injury caused by the use and application, whether directly or indirectly, of any advice or information presented, whether for breach of contract, tort, negligence, personal injury, criminal intent, or under any other cause of action.

You agree to accept all risks of using the information presented inside this book. You need to consult a professional medical practitioner in order to ensure you are both able and healthy enough to participate in this program.

TABLE OF CONTENTS

Introduction 1

Chapter 1: Scorpio Personality 4

Chapter 2: Scorpio Traits 15

Chapter 3: Scorpio Compatibility 25

Chapter 4: Scorpio Friendship 48

Chapter 5: Scorpio Woman 87

Chapter 6: Scorpioman 93

Chapter 7: Scorpio Attraction 99

Chapter 8: All Signns Aspects 108

Chapter 9: Scorpio 2021 Horoscope: Astro Predictions For The Coming Year 122

Chapter 10: Astroman Scorpio How To Charm Him, Hold Him, But Let Him Go? 141

Chapter 11: What Is Your Preferred Sexual Activity Based On Your Signification Astrological 147

Chapter 12: What Zodiac Sign Are You The Most Sexually Compatible With? 154

Chapter 13: The Main Story For The Year
.... 159

Chapter 14: Finance And Money 160

Chapter 15: Scorpio Love Match 173

Chapter 16: Scorpio Cusps 178

Introduction

Astrology is the most important factor in understanding the reasons why you and your family members are like you. It highlights your most intriguing characteristics and traits, and then explains them to you, in line with your sign. This book is not designed that teaches you the fundamentals of astrology. Instead, it's a guide for self-discovery, using Astrology as a guide. The book is intended to be put at the disposal of those who might be aware of their astrological sign, but only a little else, but want to understand how to better understand their Scorpio person. If that's you, then you've got an excellent book to your disposal.

The fascination with astrology can lead you to a great extent. You'll not only learn things about yourself but but you'll be able to view the world and people within it in various ways. You might have been contemplating the myriad of ways that people behave and function. It is possible that you thought there is no rationale or explanation to the actions of certain people. Maybe you have a close friend who is a bit cocky and temperate, or an older sibling who is shy and timid. Perhaps you have family members born within days of one their respective birth dates, and they've always seemed to be remarkably similar. Could this all be an accident? Perhaps there is something more to these events? If you are interested in Astrology, the answers may be discovered to you.

Knowing about the signs of the astrological calendar can help you gain understanding of your own life as well as the lives of other people. You'll be able discern the behaviours of other people and understand why they act in the manner they do. In all, you'll get an entire new view of the world that you've not considered previously. You may have known that you were Libra or Scorpio However, you weren't aware that this one simple name determines a lot of your life. Knowing your compatibility sign with other signs can open up a variety of doors. You may find the most significant love who the stars have destined you to meet. You can search for the most wonderful friends you'll have. It's possible to strengthen the friendships that you already have due to this greater understanding.

It doesn't matter if the fiery Leo or someone who is intuitive and emotional Cancer or a calm and calm Taurus or a powerful Aquarius If you're looking to understand more about this fascinating and fascinating concept there's no need to look further. Your personal sign is what you have. It guides you throughout your existence and in your interactions with others. If you'd like to learn more about this incredible part of the person you really are Astrology can help you understand it and much more.

Chapter 1: Scorpio Personality

Personality Profile

The main four features for the person with the sign of Scorpio are total dedication, the determination to face challenges along with their directness, and their ability to discern the truth of everything, including situations and individuals. There are many instances where Scorpio sign-signs are portrayed as attractive, sex-obsessed individuals who are flamboyantly serious and enthusiasm. Although this may be true however, it's not the entire picture, as they aren't hesitant in whatever they do. However, some signs have higher capacity to manage tasks and perform them well regardless of a lack of enthusiasm in an area When you are a

Scorpio person is enthralled by an area of study or job, there's no one who is able to dedicate their entire mind body, soul and mind to it as they do. it's the same with their relationships.

Scorpios can be focused, much like the sound of a scorpion while looking peaceful. That means that people who are angry or averse to their presence are often unaware of their actions. They're a force to be taken seriously. However their deep and of their often concealed emotions indicates that they are loyal after you have gained their trust or affection. But be sure not to violate this trust. Once a person is mistreated the Scorpio will likely never forget. Scorpios are stimulating on the inside However, they're not big on parties. Their passions aren't frivolous. There's a lot of emotion and the potential for commitment beneath the calm surface. It is likely that the Scorpio will be a serious partner in any relationship. Scorpios are also romantic and attracted to the power of. It's therefore possible that you could have to compete with an area as you would with an individual, to win the affections of the heart of a Scorpio.

Scorpios are quite confident and ambitious in any activity they want to participate in. The Scorpio sign is well-known for its inherent enthusiasm and determination. For those who are a Scorpio You approach life with an extreme enthusiasm. Because of your energy you'd prefer to be a person who's actions speak louder then your thoughts.

Scorpio Zodiac Sign

Astrologers usually consider those born between the 24th of October between November 22nd and the 24th of October being "old souls." Scorpios are usually smarter than their years. They also view the world with confidence unlike other significations. This is due in part to their distinct emotional nature. When they are in love, they love completely. If they are angry they do it with complete revenge. Although their courage is just similar to any Leo however their capacity to concentrate is superior. This means that the Scorpio an effective ally, or a feared and fierce adversary. Scorpios are known for their ability to remain calm in stressful situations. But, their tranquil exterior could conceal intense emotions. In all, Scorpio is the most private zodiac sign. This is what makes them interesting and difficult to predict.

Astrological Scorpio

The vast Scorpio constellation lies between eastern lying Libra and the eastern-facing Sagittarius. Three Greek mythologies linked this constellation to the scorpion.

One legend tells us the story of how, when Orion claimed he would destroy all animals on earth, Leto and her daughter Artemis who was a hunter but who also protected animals and sent a scorpion for protection from Orion. This scorpion took out Orion in a war that caught interest of Zeus who put the scorpion into the heavens afterward. Then , at Artemis's request, in order to remind the humans to be careful with the pride they have, Zeus added Orion on the throne of heaven.

Another myth involves an older Orion who slapped Artemis by claiming she was superior to him, which led to Artemis gaining a fling with the latter. Artemis is the twin sister of the god Apollo was furious and ordered scorpions kill Orion. Artemis asked Zeus put Orion on the sky. From that point on, Orion seeks out winter stars, but is snuffed out by the approaching of the Scorpio constellation.

A third Greek myth concerns the time when Helios the mortal son Phaeton demanded his father allow him to ride in the Sun Chariot for a single day. Helios tried to dissuade him, but Phaeton had no choice but to go for it. However, on the day he was supposed to be it was panic that was averted Phaeton which led to him losing the control of the white horses that sat in the chariot. As Phaeton was able to ascend into the sky, the world was frozen, however, he was then struck by a celestial scorpion. In fear, he brought the chariot to close the ground, igniting the vegetation, and then accidentally changing Africa into a desert, and darkening its skin. Ethiopians. To to stop this chaos Zeus struck the chariot in the runaway however Phaeton was sucked to the River Eridanos as a result.

Scorpio Temperament

Scorpios are not very fussy, being quiet introverts who are strong and preferring to focus on their work and the close circle of friends rather than overly interacting with other people to talk about socializing, gossip or even socializing. Scorpios are extremely independent, and have an unease with needing assistance from other people. Scorpios tend to work by themselves in everything they do, and when confronted with a dilemma, they turn at themselves to find the answer. Another aspect that make up the Scorpio's personality are that even though they are seeking items that are pure they're not shy about engaging in the dark side', whether it's related to sexuality , or crossing the line of what's lawful and not , or even delve into the realm of crimes themselves.

The Scorpio Child

When they are young as a child, the Scorpio is extremely attached to their parents but not in such an approach that allows them to be at peace in an exciting activity. They usually do well in school, especially in subjects they enjoy the most however, they can also excel in subjects they do not care much because of their fear of being beat in pursuit of the same goal. With louder, more aggressive siblings, a Scorpio child may be quiet at times and will fight back and defend themselves, however, this could appear as an unexpected revenge that is designed to cause the most harm. Children of Scorpio's irresponsible and naughty aspect is usually tempered through their love for family, wisdom , and their intelligence.

Scorpio Social Life

Scorpios are people who believe that any social gathering that doesn't have an adequate purpose or purpose is just a waste of time. Additionally, Scorpios can be incredibly critical and won't shy away from speaking up when something in a direct and uncoated way, regardless of regardless of whether it's related to someone's performance at work or their attitude, relationships, things or anything else. They are also extremely exact in their evaluations due to their superior level of intelligence and their natural intuition. Many people associate these tendencies with the perception of meanness and antisocial behavior that is often connected with Scorpios.

It's not like Scorpios are narcissistic or insensitive They just keep their personal side to those who are their most trusted family members and friends. They believe that everyone must be able to face the world in the way it is and be able to overcome it with no help. If you're seeking an ear to cry on You won't be able to find one with the sign of a Scorpio unless you've got really serious disasters happening at the moment that they feel empathy for. If that's the case, they'll take every step to help a friend of family member out , even when it means having to use some unconventional methods.

Ruthless Scorpio

If the relationship is with someone from the family, a friend or a romantic relationship A Scorpio is always loyal partner until you do something to them or they could quit you If they do not and they don't, their relationship will end until they find a way to take revenge on you. Additionally, Scorpios can be ruthless Although they do not typically want to be in posts with more public kinds of power. However, they can be very manipulative when it comes to achieving their goals on whatever direction they've taken in their life, refusing allow anyone to stand behind them. If someone is trying to defeat them to a certain target, or to stop them from pursuing their own route in life, working on an idea or other kind of goal, the Scorpio is not afraid of taking on their opponents head-on The challenge will only make the Scorpio fight tougher. If an Scorpio is unable to defeat their adversaries then they'll wait for their next opportunity to take revenge in the future.

Love Relationships

In a room, in the presence of a Scorpio is sure to draw the attention of the people in the vicinity with their magnetic appeal. This attraction is due to their impressive presence, their capacity to achieve what they want out of people and their enigma. You'll never fully understand the Scorpio within your life, because they aren't one to talk about or reveal their most intimate feelings, regardless of how much they cherish you. They'll just give you the information they believe you should be aware of and nothing more. You shouldn't think this is a sign of the Scorpio not love them you can be sure that If they didn't love them, then they would not want them within their world. However, it may take time for an Scorpio to allow you to become an integral part of their life, from being a person who takes everything crucial to them seriously and being thrilled by life's difficulties (with love being just one of them) The Scorpio makes for a great long-term companion as they're extremely loyal and due to their sharp sense, they are aware of what their loved ones require and are committed to addressing their demands.

Flower Sign...Chrysanthemum

The claim to fame "My existence is one of puzzle and mystery"

The chrysanthemum flower is a multifaceted person. Even when you feel like others hold you down to the wall, you take an animal from your hat. Being honest and open is essential to be able to interact with anyone. The majority of the time when something gets tense or unpleasant, you are able to make an entrance to cleanse the scene and help in the healing of any wounds that have recently occurred. The chrysanthemum is able to pinpoint their lives and firmly identifies imperfections, taking stock of all the emotions that love. While it can be a bit unsettling, the chrysanthemum's sensitivity is a great way to help others to overcome their weaknesses or shortcomings. Additionally, there is no shortage of flowers and there is the future is bright for lovers who are with you.

Famous Scorpios Include:

Albert Camus, Bill Gates, Billy Connelly, Bjork, Bo Derek, Bryan Adams, Calvin Klein, Charles Bronson, Claude Rains, Demi Moore, Ethan Hawke, Famke Janssen, Gerard Butler, Grace Kelly, Jeremy London, Jamie Lee Curtis, Larry King, Marie Curie, Marlene Dietrich, Meg Ryan, Napolean Hill, Owen Wilson, Pablo Picasso, Peter Cook, Peter Jackson, Richard Burton, Ricky Martin, Ryan Gosling, Sally Field, Scarlett Johansson, Voltaire, Veronica Lake, Winona Ryder.

Chapter 2: Scorpio Traits

Personality Profile

As Scorpions like to degrade their prey before taking it to eat or killing the animal, Scorpios also tend to keep grudges against another person and contemplate ways they can get revenge, instead of expressing outrage. They are also naturally curious. They believe that what's concealed is more interesting than what is obvious. They are also strong women and women, and not the ones to shun potential adversaries who could be mighty.

However, they seldom attack from the front. Instead, Scorpio signs are patiently waiting for the perfect time to strike and strike at the exact moment you least would. Despite this, Scorpios also exhibit a many positive qualities. They are intelligent, diplomatic and resolute. They are also intuitive engaged, sensitive and spiritual. Despite their power, Scorpios are regarded as an inactive sign of the zodiac. They're also known as for being egocentric, but that's not to say the do not have an charitable aspect to them.

Zodiac Scorpio

People born between October 23- November 21 are into the role of Scorpio which is symbolized by the powerful and deadly scorpion. Scorpio represents the eight zodiac sign and most astrologers believe Scorpio to be an introverted feminine sign. Scientists find studying Scorpio very interesting due to their personality is diverse. They're both fascinating and risky. Astrologers categorize Scorpios into three types:

Positivous: Insane and horrible, they'll keep an unresolved grudge for a long period of time and will continue to plan their revenge and then take it out at the earliest chance.

Noble: Selfless and rational. The Scorpio significators have learned to manage their emotions with rational thought and are more likely to respond more effectively to offenses committed to them.

Lizards Scorpios which are classified as lizards are generally harmless, however they could be dangerous in certain instances, when they choose to. The way to judge their intentions may be challenging.

Scorpio as water Sign

Scorpio is an astrologically significant water sign. Like other water signs, they're extremely emotional. They can differ in intensity from the shallows to deeper, based on the circumstances they're faced with. Like sea creatures, Scorpios hold many secrets and possess an air of mystery about their appearance. They are known to hide their true feelings behind a seeming calm and serene appearance however, you should never believe that they are innocent. Scorpios are creatures that plot and may have a plan to harm you should you come into contact with them.

Positive Strengths and Qualities

If you are in the love of someone, Scorpios are the most trustworthy people you'll encounter. They have a strong will and will do all they can to reach their goals regardless of what it requires. They are willing to sacrifice everything for the woman or man they love, but they may also be a bit insecure with their family members. Some people are drawn to them because of their magnetic personality. Many refer to them as natural leaders, being the dominant personalities they are.

Characteristics that distinguish Scorpios from other signs of the zodiac is their extreme love and devotion to family, friends or love ones. They are extremely passionate about their love for others and are extremely supportive and generous, as so long as you don't harm their feelings. Scorpios also have a captivating personality. They are lively and smart speakers who hold your attention for long durations of time. They are charming and funny and are very pleasant people to hang out with.

Negative Qualities and weaknesses

Scorpio signs are possessive, to the detriment of their personal relationships. They can be extremely jealous and without reason. They are obsessed with small and unimportant things. They can be manipulative and headstrong shaping things and situations to favor them, even if they know the truth. They can also be quite emotional and can lose their temper quickly, which is why they are prone to conflicts and miscommunication frequently. It can be difficult to trust people right from the start.

Scorpio are vindictive and revengeful they never forget a minor or a mistake that is easily. They are able to hold grievances for a long period of time, and then wait until the right time to take action. Scorpios are not averse to confrontation, preferring to plan and manipulate people, things and their environment using skillful tactics to reach their objectives.

Specific characteristics of Scorpio

dominant: Scorpios have a very dominating individuals in their personal and professional lives. They are powerful and strong which is that are evident through their management.

The Scorpio sign is a danger: they make excellent companions, but they are also terrible enemies. It is certain they'll strike back and hurt you with their poisonous "tit to tat". Be careful when you play with Scorpios the way you would do with scorpions.

Attractive: In general Scorpios are attractive physically and most are magnetic. This is why people are attracted to Scorpios. This helps make them great leaders, they can be prone to ego issues if it becomes too much of a concern.

The Temperamental Scorpio Zodiac significations are unpredictable, changing their moods fast enough that even their closest family and friends have a hard time predicting their mood. If they change in a negative way, the people who are around them will choose not to interact with their friends during the time.

Sturdy: Scorpios truly are stubborn whether for worse. If they are determined to accomplish something, they'll accomplish it in any way. This is what can make them successful. However If they've made their minds on something, they can persuade them to change their mind or convince them.

Scorpio Career

Scorpios are clever and smart that allow them to excel in any field they pick. Their drive to discover the dark makes them experts of the zodiac and they can excel as investigators and detectives. Scorpios are also incredibly insightful and are excellent spiritual healers as well as holistic doctors. Their wisdom also allows them to succeed as PMs and leaders in politics.

Scorpio Compatibility

Leo as well as Scorpio compatibility usually starts out with great energy, however, the attraction fades in time, but it rarely proves to be a negative one. In the same way, Aries and Scorpio compatibility will likely to be strong at first but could be to be destined for trouble in the long run since both be decisive rather than just muttering words. If the Scorpio is quiet or tolerant, a compassionate Cancer could turn out to be a great companion. Virgo as well as Scorpio compatibility is extremely poor as both be adamant about their personalities, however they have distinct objectives and perspectives about the world. Two Scorpios are a terrible combination due to their dominant nature . Sagittarius as well as Scorpio are doomed due to the fact that Sagittarius is always keen to be active while Scorpios like to be at home. However, Aquarius and Scorpio are compatible, it starts slowly but it becomes volatile and explosive because of the peaceful nature that is Scorpio as well as the open character of Aquarius. Scorpio and Taurus - The Scorpio is extremely demanding deeply emotional, and intimate.

The Scorpions are the 'tough people' of the zodiac. The word "stiff" refers to they are looking to be heard but not to be questioned. They strive to be different in all that they do. If they put their minds on something, their view of it will remain as it is. It's impossible to alter their opinions. Scorpios love secrets like little treasures. Although they're very private in nature, they don't want anyone else to believe that they are guilty of anything. They are adept at securing information who know exactly what they can do to obtain the information they need to get from their peers. The Scorpions are stubborn and possess a strong desire to be successful in their the workplace and in relationships. It's not in the nature of the Scorpion to cheat on their partner. And they aren't likely to commit to a long-term commitment in the first place if they've never fully made the decision their own.

The Scorpions, both male and female, are also extremely practical. They don't have many of them in the cloud. They are extremely self-aware having a good understanding of their strengths as they are aware of their weaknesses, and therefore aren't enticed by empty flattery or are enthralled by it. Injustice and unfairness bother them as well. Scorpios are a serious lot. Because they possess a powerful desire to achieve success in key areas of life, they are with a lot of passion to reach their goals and will go to extreme measures to achieve these goals.

They are steadfast in their goal and will not sacrifice or compromise to complete the job. They are dedicated workers and perfectionists as they wish to be able to look back and affirm that they are satisfied with the work they've done. Their way of relationships and their lives are so constant that the frivolous or shallow people who aren't prepared to deal with the intensity and commitment of this group should not apply. This intense nature of Scorpio individuals can only be endured long enough due to their regenerative abilities which allow them to recover easily from disappointments and setbacks similar to the insect scorpion rapidly regenerating the tail after losing its old one.

Because Scorpios are naturally stubborn They are known for dominant with their loved ones and friends. However, all of this is a result of a deep feeling of love and love for the few people they've been devoted to and protect at all times throughout their lives. As the Scorpion you are a committed driven, dedicated, and a diligent person who is dedicated for your cause. You contribute 100 and one per cent of your sweat, blood and tears, never ever stopping until you have it perfect to your eyes. You are adamant about honesty and want to earn it from others. If there's one thing you can't resist, it's being cheated, betrayed or being just let down. It is possible to distinguish flattery from genuine praise because you know your own self.

Chapter 3: Scorpio Compatibility

Scorpio Compatibility

	Compatibility	Sex	Communication
Aries	XX	XXX	XX
Taurus	XXX	XXX	XXX
Gemini	X	XX	X
Cancer	XXX	XXX	XXX
Leo	XX	XXX	X
Virgo	XXX	XXX	X
Libra	XX	XX	X
Scorpio	XXX	XXX	XX
Sagittarius	X	XX	X
Capricorn	XXX	XXX	XXX
Aquarius	XX	XX	X
Pisces	XXX	XXX	XXX

Compatibility Profile

Scorpio is generally thought of as possibly the most intense astrology sign, even to the point of the level of. But this isn't quite the case. It's true that Scorpio is never a person to be judged by the half. They may be equally passionate about what they perform, the research they pursue, or an interest they are interested in. It doesn't relate to the activities inside the home. But, don't think that the Scorpio to become a social animal. They prefer a smaller circle of close friends over a vast amount of friends. They're very similar to Gemini in this respect however they are more concerned about stimulating their minds than simply having fun. Scorpios are stimulating to be around but their commitment to enthusiasm can be a hindrance under certain circumstances.

Aries with Scorpio

Scorpio or Aries are extremely passionate individuals and have a powerful desire to live a full life. It is also something they cherish about each other. The couple is fiery within their relationships, and fights are frequently violent. Aries is known to let their emotions out, and then forget about it later. Scorpio However, they will retain resentments similar to those Aries tends to inflict on them. Scorpio is adamant to feel a strong emotional connection with another; Aries doesn't share this sensation.

Both Aries and Scorpio respond with a lot of force to the environment and to individuals. But how they express their emotions can differs. Aries are often easily annoyed and angry; they are often prone to short-lived tempers. Scorpio conceals their emotions and can be a bit irritable for a lengthy time. Scorpio is usually sensitive, secretive, and difficult to understand. When it comes down to loving or despising an individual, they do so in their entire heart. Aries is more clear in their approach, but may not fully comprehend how deep the emotions of Scorpio can be.

There could be some disagreements between the couple, but they're bound by their love. Scorpio is a lover of their partner: affection, emotional commitment along with emotional depth. Scorpio isn't one to take things at their true value and as a result, Scorpio is always looking into the person's emotions. This could lead to them having problems. There is no doubt about how drawn the two types of signs are one another. They could have a genuine bond if they recognize each other's methods of thinking.

Taurus with Scorpio

Taurus and Scorpio are in a close relationship towards one another. even when there is no connection that goes beyond physical, the physical may be intense and hold them in a close relationship. If they share desires and both are able to connect on an intellectual level, the capacity to remain together is powerful. Both signs are very self-centered, with Scorpio having moments of jealousy. Their psychological makeups differ significantly: Taurus tends to be relatively simple and doesn't require anyone as much as Scorpio is. Scorpio seeks a profound emotional connection, more that Taurus does. Both are extremely stubborn and both require ways to work together in order to get along romantically. They are not able to talk effectively about the things that are important to them and can result in huge misunderstandings.

Once they have their minds set that they're in whether Scorpio or Taurus. It doesn't matter whether something is rational or sensible, particularly when they're looking for something. When these signs meet it's the moment to determine which is the first to cave. Taurus is the sign that is more pragmatic and more earthy. Taurus prefer an enviable, tranquil life at home, and is known to enjoy a positive emotional side to their lives. Actually, this is a sign that is easily happy. The emotions of Scorpio are often intense and, as a result they are able to be deeply in love or hate. Scorpios tend to hide the innermost parts of themselves and be withdrawn from others to protect themselves. The emotions that Scorpio keep hidden areanger, jealousy and anger. Taurus is often astonished regarding the Scorpio however, they have a sense of ownership towards their companion.

Gemini with Scorpio

An Gemini or Scorpio couple is as different as day and night. Scorpio can be emotionally connected on a deeper degree, particularly with regards to settings and people. Scorpio develops a strong bond , and is often connected to others, particularly their love. Gemini However, they take life with some caution and isn't as bonded emotionally as Scorpio. This is the reason Scorpio considers Gemini as an elusive and childlike person who's not very serious. Gemini perceives Scorpio as overly demanding, intense, someone who is simply a glutton. Scorpio is a great choice for very intense, immediate experiences. their life is most enjoyable when things are simple and non-intellectual, and allow the use of their hands. Gemini is a lover of many things, and is less concentrated. Their approach to life could be different too. Thus they will have to cooperate in order to work through their differences and not cause them distress. The truth about their attraction to one another is that the traits which make them unique draw them in.

In terms of the emotional characteristics of Gemini and Scorpio their differences are so great that the two have difficulty getting to know and appreciate each other. Scorpio is very emotionally driven and can feel things at a deep level. If it's about responding to situations, they can show strong feelings of hatred or love for the things they are passionate about. As such, is not equipped with the ability of a Gemini to be rational or intelligent when it comes to personal issues.

In terms of situations, Gemini takes things lightly and cool. Scorpio can be a bit heavy-handed with a strong emotional nature. Actually, Gemini takes things so easy it is Scorpio claims they aren't caring an inch or any emotions at all. Gemini is not comfortable with their emotions and is using denial to avoid the intensity Scorpio experiences.

Gemini enjoys being around people, and often seeks out things that provide them with the opportunity to be creative or provide mental stimulation. Scorpio is a more individual, and is regarded as being unsociable. Gemini prefers the freedom to travel, but Scorpio dislikes the other interests and relationships that Gemini is able to enjoy. Scorpio is a person who has a need to connect with others in a intimate way which makes them a demanding sign. They are looking for the same from Gemini that's why they might not get.

Cancer and Scorpio

Cancer and Scorpio along with their natural tendency to be close and bond deeply, are able to are able to connect quickly and effortlessly. They are alike in their attitudes and goals. However, there are some distinctions between these signs. Cancer has a great deal of sentimental empathy and compassion for other people however Scorpio is averse to these feelings and views Cancer as too romantic. If they're wounded, Cancer tends to have an attitude of resentment. Cancer is known to sulk or retreat away from the world when they're wounded. They let the other person know exactly how they feel. They do this in a non-verbal way. Scorpio conceals their hurt.

The two signs also display their feelings towards love and sexuality in a different way. Cancer has a tendency to believe Scorpio isn't motivated through love but the urge to lust and desire. This could be a problem for the couple. The intense bond between the couple and their emotional state may strengthen the bond between them. The two Cancer and Scorpio will have a more easy time with intimacy. They'll be more comfortable in comparison to other families. Both view loyalty as a crucial aspect to them.

Both are sensitive and intuitive about the feelings and needs of others; they are emotionally connected to others. The connection among Cancer as well as Scorpio is very strong; it's a bond that's founded on the emotional value. Cancer relies on their loved ones and although Scorpio also has a dependency but they don't always know or acknowledge their dependence. If both signets are attached to somebody or desire something, they could lose their impartiality.

Although the compatibility between the two is apparent however, there are some distinctions between the two. Scorpio is very passionate and has strong emotions toward people and situations. This includes their love and hatred. It's rare that Scorpio is open about their feelings and vulnerabilities as a result they're not able to surrender control of the course of a relationship. Scorpio is a person who, when they're angry or hurt is prone to be extremely violent. Cancer is more subdued in its way of life and is often irritated by the fury Scorpio exhibits. Cancer is looking for a space that is calming and soothing.

Leo with Scorpio

Both are determined and stubborn; a character characteristic that both can sense from one another. The conquest feeling is usually more intense whenever there's excitement the relationship. But both of these strong willed personalities can cause problems in long-term relationships. Because of the rigid nature of Scorpio and Leo they are unable for a couple to arrive at an arrangement that is acceptable to both. It is difficult to negotiate compromises when there's a divergence in their preferences. It is likely that there will be the battle of the wills. Another issue that could arise between the two couples is jealousy. Scorpio is a sign that is very intensely connected and is a lover of monogamy. While Leo is a faithful the sign is not the intensity Scorpio offers.

Leo and Scorpio's personalities are like the day and night - Leo is friendly and warm The sign that is a lover of having fun. Scorpio is a quiet type with a strong emotional connection in the world and is difficult to understand. Scorpio is a shrewd soul and more so than Leo. In the midst of that emotions and sensitivity, is Scorpio always seeking the more profound side of people and the meaning behind their words. They also seek to know about the past and the hidden aspect of an individual. Leo is open to things and is often convinced that Scorpio's invasiveness is not a good thing.

Leo is an extremely proud sign and would like to be viewed in a positive terms. They do not want being seen as a different type of light. Scorpio is jealous and is wary of Leo's open personality and they simply aren't able to comprehend. Leo may become annoyed due to the suspicions of Scorpio.

Scorpio is attracted to the mystery of life. Leo searching for the good things. Leo is a social person with a need to entertain. Scorpio prefers time at home, in a quiet environment with only a couple of companions. This is why the conversation is usually deep and intimate. If there is trust and understanding that there is no struggle or disagreements between the two. They both are inflexible at times , and insist to be who they are regardless of differences.

Virgo with Scorpio

Scorpio and Virgo are the Scorpio as well as the Virgo pair share very similar temperaments, having the same desire to examine objects and people, as well as an ability to remain calm. They also take a more inner reflection on the difficulties life can throw at them. There are instances that Scorpio is prone to slipping into situations without hesitation, while the Virgo adopts a cautious approach. Scorpio frequently thinks of Virgo as a timid person, whereas the Virgo perceives the Scorpio as being impulsive and reckless. There are many situations where the Scorpio is seen as more stubborn than Virgo and could think of the Virgo's lack dedication as weak points. Virgo is inclined to view Scorpio as being too emotionally involved and dependent on ideas or circumstances. Virgo is highly sensitive and has sensibilities that require keeping their hands and bodies clean. Scorpio isn't afraid to get dirty and dirty. Even though their personality traits are different they want harmony in their relationship...not to cause conflict between them. With the similar approach to life, they usually accomplish this.

Scorpio is a peaceful and quiet character that is deeply complicated with hidden emotions and strong emotions like shame, jealousy, and shame. Scorpio requires passion and awe to be alive within. It is intentional or not, it is likely to trigger some kind of storm that creates these emotions. Scorpio can be negative in a sense, is a manipulative and manipulative. However, on the positive side they are loyal and loyal. Virgo isn't like Scorpio as they prefer to react to events with a rational approach and not based on instinct. Virgo is the reserved more reserved sign especially when it comes down to matters of a sexual or emotional nature. Virgo frequently does not comprehend Scorpio's strong emotions. Virgo can be a sensitive person. So, Scorpio should be cautious not to become too serious in order to avoid causing discomfort for the Virgo. The two Virgo and Scorpio frequently take a look at themselves with a critical eye and have a strong desire to alter the way they perceive themselves, typically to their advantage.

Libra along with Scorpio

There are situations in which Scorpio responds with greater emotional energy than Libra. Even though Libra isn't considered to be an insecure sign, the emotions Scorpio can feel tend to be deeper. Both desire a close relationship. Yet, Scorpio can become too focused on a single particular person or object; Libra can keep themselves in a distance from other people, even when they're married. Libra lives life with a sense of harmony, while Scorpio has a strong desire to connect. Scorpio tends to be obsessed with things they believe to be worried about. The Libran's attitude of fairness detached could be a source of anger for the Scorpio. Libra is often confused by Scorpio's moodiness. The distinct personalities of both aren't usually a cause for concern in their relationship. The emotional bonds between two are often robust, particularly in the event that there are other ties connecting them.

Libra is the most social sign with a personable manner that others appreciate. Libra likes to be with others and has an urge to be associated in pleasant environments. They aren't a fan of dealing with a host of arguments or anger within their relationships. Scorpio typically is less tense and have a deeper emotional complexity in their. They do not like conversations that are light in any way; often they are lonely in situations such as this.

Scorpio is a person who experiences a variety of emotions like jealousy, desire and rage, hate and love. Scorpio cannot function without a sense of intimate relationship in their lives and can involve conflicts and confrontations. If the atmosphere is too calm and calm, Scorpio is known to cause tension, sometimes with intent but sometimes not. Libra prefers an enlightened environment to be in. Scorpio tends to gravitate towards the negative side of life and people. Libra seeks out the good in people. Libra is more likely to take people for what they are, while Scorpio prefers to look into an individual. So, Scorpio may imperceptibly try to control in a relationship.

Scorpio with Scorpio

This bond can be intense, frequently creating a love affair with each other. A love affair this intense frequently can lead to union. The reason for this is that both partners are heavily towards a commitment. They don't like a casual relationship and find it difficult to feel like they are "dating" in an informal manner. Both would prefer to be totally engaged in their relationship or not have any kind of relationship even. They can be extremely possessive of one another. As with the majority of relationship, this Scorpio/Scorpio union can be difficult. The most common issues to anticipate from this relationship are arguments and violent reunions. Although the couple is extremely passionate about each other but they also hate each other equally. The relationship can be satisfying or absolutely destructive. there is no middle ground in this scenario.

It's no secret that the Scorpio/Scorpio alliance is extremely passionate and volatile. Both of them have an intense passion that they feel deeply and rarely share with anyone other than those who they have a close relationship with. The emotional reactions can be extreme. The

Scorpio is a victim of love, hate affection, loyalty, hatred and so on. all in one swift single swoop. In the absence of releasing their feelings all at once, all in one swoop. Scorpio may ponder the subject for hours and then a rise in guilt or resentment are frequently noticed. Both Scorpios are apprehensive about privacy and make sure that things remain kept secret; secrets are a delight to this pair. Because both Scorpios are highly sceptical of divulging their identity when they are asked to disclose who they are, it's because they trust one another very much. Betrayal and jealousy are often experienced by this sign as well.

Due to the Scorpio couple's similar their nature, they can understand each other very well. If they disagree and then explode, it can be quite significant. Both Scorpios are drawn to strong emotional connections, and are always searching for them in various ways. Certain of these include extremely risky or challenging physical tasks, or working in a risky career, watching or reading a horror film or creating terror within their own lives.

Sagittarius paired with Scorpio

Sagittarius and Scorpio can be quite different. Sagittarius is usually excited about dreams, plans and projects. In addition, they consider Scorpio as too stubborn to be able to accept these kinds of plans. Sagittarius is a social butterfly, while Scorpio does not feel comfortable in a group setting with large numbers of people. Scorpio is able to put in lots of energy in activities; Sagittarius prefers doing little parts of everything and participating in a variety of interests and activities. Scorpio's emotions tend to be deeper than those of Sagittarius due to this Sagittarius is not able to comprehend Scorpio's emotions and experiences.

Scorpio can be very emotional particularly with their loved ones and dislikes the thought of sharing the affection and emotions of Sagittarius with anyone other than them. Sagittarius is somewhat of a flirt, and may effortlessly provoke the jealousy that is Scorpio. Sagittarius may be overwhelmed by the suspicion of the Scorpio who is looking for their loyalty. The most difficult part is that Sagittarius is often unable to meet the Scorpio's demands without even realizing how powerful they feel. Sagittarius is a person who needs independence. The signs of

Sagittarius are very different and require an understanding of the two to truly be the perfect couple.

Sagittarius Scorpio and Scorpio are very different emotionally. Sagittarius is optimistic and is always seeking ways to conquer any negative moment in their lives. The sign is often oblivious to the darker, more sombre aspects of life and the emotions. Scorpio is a intense person who can't disconnect from other people or objects.

The Sagittarius sign is one of the most open; Scorpio doesn't trust people and is very cautious. Scorpio is a quiet person who may socialize occasionally. But, Sagittarius is not the kind of person who enjoys socializing with others. Scorpio can be quiet, before becoming sad and depressing. Sagittarius take every opportunity to brighten their mood. Sagittarius likes to see the positive side of things; Scorpio loves the storms.

Scorpio is very connected to their beloved and, when that relationship gets strained, they are more sensitive to the situation. A few of the emotional problems Scorpio is prone to are possessiveness and jealousy. Sagittarius isn't a possessive type of person. Instead, they are generous emotionally. They are looking for the freedom to be able to take care of themselves without the constant scrutiny Scorpio puts on them.

Capricorn with Scorpio

Both Capricorn and Scorpio must be cautious when it comes time to reveal their fears, feelings, and motives, particularly in the event that neither of them wants to reveal the deepest aspects of themselves. Both sign signs have a tough to trust. Both of them are naturally cautious and shy. In regards in relationships, both are typically kept at a distance. The main difference in Capricorn Scorpio and Scorpio can be seen in the way that Capricorn is able to remain objective as well as detached from their emotions; much more than Scorpio. Capricorn tends to be distant particularly when they feel at risk. Scorpio is often apathetic to their feelings. Scorpio is extremely passionate and will be deeply be in love with their loved ones. Capricorns may not feel the same deeply, but even the case, they will not display how deep their love extends. This isn't the kind of relationship that's fun.

Both are fairly quiet, they are not signs that let their emotions in a public manner. However, the motives for being unable to express feelings differ for each. Capricorn is a person who tries to suppress their emotions; typically, they're not content playing the inner child that'd prefer to be cared for their priorities on work and practical matters. with their desire to have fun and play controlled. Capricorn frequently ignores their childish desires. They usually keep their heads away from the world from being engaged emotionally. Capricorns are often indifferent or indifferent and tends to be a bit too serious about life. Their only option for happiness is material security and success.

Scorpio is extremely emotional However, they tend to keep their emotions. The Scorpio sign is very complex and keeps feelings in check for a considerable period of time. If you're feeling guilty or feeling bitter, Scorpio can build these emotions if they're not let go. They are not able to trust easily and fear not having control, which stops them from expressing their feelings to one another completely. Both can provide significant consistency and depth to the relationship, without having any apparent feelings. That's why the two mix well.

Aquarius with Scorpio

Aquarius is an optimist. Scorpio tends to be more dependent on their intuition, relying to their gut reaction and emotions. Aquarius is astonished by Scorpio's intense love/hate emotions since they're considered to be the sensible sign. Scorpio has also been emotionally connected to their loved one, becoming fixed on one particular person. Aquarius is, on the contrary, is more aloof. They are in need of multiple friends and aren't keen on getting too personal. This can create emotional gap between the two and could be difficult to overcome. Both of these signs are uncompromising and highly opinionated. If a relationship that lasts for a long time is in the cards the couple must overcome their differences and respect each other more.

The emotions and needs of Scorpio as well as Aquarius are similar to day and night. That's the difference between them. Because of this the two signs frequently argue until they are able to be able to come to a common understanding and accept each other for who they are. The issue is that both of them are established in their beliefs and do not like change until the change is made in the manner they prefer. Scorpio seeks intimacy and affection which is why they are often attached to those they like. They have to master the art of gaining control over their manipulative, jealous and possessive emotions in order to be able to enjoy an "normal" relation. Aquarius dislikes being restricted or being manipulated and is resistant to any type of apprehension of their loved ones. Additionally Aquarius is more of a person with a mental outlook than they are emotional.

Scorpio lets emotions be a major factor in their lives. Because of this, they're focused on their emotions and their desires. Aquarius is more detached way of handling life, usually not being in touch with their emotions and emotions. Actually, Scorpio is often met by the cool personality of Aquarius who are unable to be able to comprehend Scorpio's ways of thinking. Scorpio is an extremely private individual. Aquarius is more social and enjoys being part of the world. They are more likely to be active in organizations, community events and clubs. Aquarius Aquarius has a variety of interests and requires stimulation of the mind; something that Scorpio isn't likely to provide.

Pisces along with Scorpio

Both sign types are intensely passionate, with strong emotions and are very sensitive. They actually are in a deep emotional bond that is shared with trust in intimate relationships. The loving, non-judgmental disposition of Pisces can be soothing for the Scorpio that has a tendency to carry an abundance of hurt, guilt and internal conflicts. Scorpio tends to be more aggressive than Pisces and can be a bit more violent, expressing aggression that can hurt the self-esteem of Pisces. Pisces isn't protected by this armor, and is more gentle in their character. Pisces is a more gentle and loving sign. Pisces and Scorpio character is different in the sense that Pisces is a lover of romanticism and subtleties, whereas Scorpio is more sexual and physical. But, the relationship of Scorpio and Pisces is very compatible and may be extremely satisfying.

Both are highly psychically sensitive and can sense what others feel, even if they are to cover it up. This kind of connection can make a difference for both. Furthermore, because they are so absorbed it is difficult for them to discern if the emotions they experience are truly their personal. Though they're sensitive in their nature, their signs differ. Scorpio holds on to emotions, guilt and fears for a considerable period. Pisces is more accepting and accepting; however, when they are offended they'll still find excuses for the person. Scorpio is a fighter , and when injured they're not afraid to take revenge. Pisces is a peaceful sign that isn't a fan of fighting. While they are sensitive at a deeper level of emotion however, they're not terribly open about their personal experiences and feelings. They have a passion for music. Living near water can be beneficial to both.

Chapter 4: Scorpio Friendship

Friendship Profile

The mysterious Scorpion could become the most loyal friend you've ever experienced -- or perhaps your most formidable foe. The most important rule to follow with the Scorpio is to should never do anything to them. They are stingy and they will never forget the wrongs caused to them. It's simple to ensure that your Scorpio relationship intact. And once you show that you're worthy of their love They will become an unwavering ally. It is impossible to know what's going on in their minds. You may not be aware what your position is However, their secrets will never cease to captivate you. Kissing is a huge distasteful for your Scorpion friend and you should be sure to tell them how amazing they are, but don't fawning over them.

Scorpio is not a person with many acquaintances, but they are loyal to the ones they do have. Friendship isn't the only important aspect of the lives of Scorpios, however they remain loyal to a partner for a long time. A Scorpio will be willing to offer you a shirt off their back in case you require it, but you could be able to sense they may have a motive for doing this. The relationship with the Scorpion is always filled with unexpected surprises.

Best Bets for Friends: Virgo, Capricorn

Aries and Scorpio

If Aries and Scorpio become friends They'll be left wondering what they did to get along. Both are strong and, if they can learn to co-exist instead of fighting with each other, they'll be able to accomplish anything they wish to achieve. Scorpio has more focus and determined than Aries and Aries can get things going with the same way they desire. Although Aries is a loyal sign, Scorpio has a deeper and more intricate commitment to relationship.

It can be a focused relationship. It is typically emotional and often a bit argumentative due to the fact that each Aries and Scorpio are prone to jealousy. Scorpio is more patient, but it is also more affluent than Aries. Although they have their own differences, both are prone to taking risks; this isn't a boring love affair! Aries and Scorpio may have many adventures together. At times, they may be unable to understand each other as Aries tends to be an outgoing outgoing and open and open, whereas Scorpio is more reserved in their emotions. Both of them need to get together at least every once in awhile and make a truce!

Aries as well as Scorpio are both controlled by the Planet Mars, and Scorpio is also one of the planets ruled by Pluto. When two people who have Mars energy unite and are able to communicate, it's like two soldiers on an arena: They're either allies or adversaries. Mars is also a symbol of enthusiasm, and so Aries and Scorpio are likely to enjoy a fun time. They both face challenges head-on, which is why it's common for them to fight constantly and making up is something you can anticipate! Pluto brings a new vigor to this energy.

Aries is an Fire Sign and Scorpio is water-based Sign. Both of them can make an ideal combination when they are able to work together by using physical and emotional action to achieve goals. Scorpio is a skilled strategist, and can aid Aries to slow down their pace and discover how to plan battles prior to engaging in the fight.

Aries helps Scorpio learn to relax and let go when their attempts are unsuccessful. Scorpio can be manipulative emotionally with too much Water, which can dampen Aries their fiery passion. However, too much fire could burn the Water away, and cause Scorpio to pursue revenge. Aries and Scorpio need to learn the two c's of life -collaboration and compromisewhen they are concerned enough about one another and their relationship to keep their equilibrium.

Aries is a Cardinal Sign. Scorpio is an Fixed Sign. Aries provides Scorpio the freedom to take on things for fun instead of always having an agenda. Scorpio is a stabilizing force for Aries by influencing their playful friend to finish something before launching into something completely new. Both are committed and loyal to each other, and when they realize that they are both the chiefs, Aries as the initiator and Scorpio as the emotional leader, they are able to be friends and enjoy many enjoyable moments.

The greatest benefit of the Aries-Scorpio relationship is the strength of their forces. They can accomplish a lot accomplished, especially when they're committed to the common cause. They're both winners and will never quit, creating an alliance that never settles for less than the top.

Taurus and Scorpio

If Taurus and Scorpio create a bond The result is two opposite signs in the Zodiac merging, the result is a blend of two halves. Polarity signs like those often form an entire, with each of the strengths and weaknesses balancing each other. The signs of polarity usually have a strong attraction toward one another and when they're together, the tension can be intense! Taurus Scorpio and Taurus Scorpio have plenty in common, however due to their strong personalities to their friendship, the tone of the conversation often changes from excitement to fervent disagreement!

Taurus and Scorpio are both keen on working together towards getting things: Taurus wants material goods and Scorpio seeks power. Both signs are interested in riches and resources, such as the inheritance tax and other taxes. They're both committed to all aspects of their lives. They complement one another due to the fact that Taurus is more focused on self-interest, while Scorpio is more about the immediate family, which includes family. In addition, Taurus is more direct and direct, whereas Scorpio is a mystery. Due to their distinct characteristics each sign can develop and learn from one another -or when they are able to compromise.

Taurus is controlled by Venus as well as Scorpio is controlled by Mars and Pluto. This is a very powerful combination because of the influence of Pluto and influence, yet it's a healthy combination of feminine and masculine energy. Two signs that are in sync create the basis of human relations -that is Venus is love, as well as Mars's passion. Venus and Mars are compatible; Venus is about beauty and Mars is all about passion. Scorpio is passionate, and Taurus is drawn to this passion. In turn, Scorpio enjoys the devotion that is a part of Venus-ruled Taurus.

Taurus can be described as one of the Earth Sign, and Scorpio is the Water Sign. Scorpio is a deep sign. It's an ocean and too much turmoil could result in a tsunami! Scorpio's emotional receding and retreats but then roars back with the rage of. Taurus as well as Scorpio are extremely committed to one another due to their shared need to be secure in their emotional lives. When Taurus is open and has everything exposed to the naked eye, Scorpio is more focused on the inner workings of life. Scorpio is able to show Taurus beyond the superficial as well as Taurus is able to teach Scorpio to speak with more honesty. In addition, Scorpio appreciates the Taurus practicality and Taurus is a fan of Scorpio's jealousy. this proves they're loved.

Taurus as well as Scorpio Are both fixed signs. If they share a common aim, nothing will stand in their way. If the views of the two friends are different however, a firestorm could occur! It is often the case that Taurus is the dominant sign but this isn't always the situation. Sometimes Scorpio isn't even willing to disagree, even though they might appear to be willing to compromise and then retaliate through manipulating their emotions. It's crucial for the members to discuss what's essential to them, so they can find an agreement that is fair. When Scorpio is able to believe in Taurus and comprehend the significance of friendship" They can accomplish anything with pure determination. The relationship is only going to be a failure if the two can't overcome their opinions rigid side.

The greatest benefit of the Taurus-Scorpio relationship is their strong cooperation when they can agree on the goals they want to achieve. When Scorpio recognizes that Taurus is in the long run and won't bring the angst that Scorpios are attracted to in their lives, their friendship will blossom. Their common determination forms a strong bond.

Gemini and Scorpio

If Gemini and Scorpio discover the joy in their differences They can form an alliance that's an element to be faced with. The Scorpion is focused, and determined than Gemini while Gemini can be easily adapted and more social than Scorpio. Scorpions have a strong loyalty to their friends, whereas Gemini is more comfortable with life generally. They each have their own objectives, but if they cooperate, they'll accomplish anything.

It can be a focus-oriented relationship. Gemini is often highly emotional and often a bit argumentative due to the fact that Scorpio has a lust for jealousy and Gemini may appear to be not caring. Gemini also enjoys arguing simply for the sake of it. Scorpio is more patient, but also more protective than Gemini. However, they are have a love of risk and taking risks. This isn't a boring friendship! Gemini and Scorpio can enjoy a variety of adventures. At times, they may be unable to understand each other due to the fact that Gemini can be known as an extrovert in the front and outgoing while Scorpio is more obscure. Both require a seat at the bargaining table time and come up with an agreement on peace!

Gemini governs Planet Mercury, and Scorpio is ruled by both the planets Mars as well as Pluto. Gemini's great communication skills help to help to avert the tension that could be triggered by the smoldering and sometimes difficult to reach Scorpio. Mars is also a symbol of enthusiasm, which is why Scorpio's energy can make for an energetic and thrilling time. Both love challenges, and a the heated debate won't scare away either of them. Making up is more fun! Pluto is a great addition in this lively dynamic.

Gemini can be described as an air Sign and Scorpio is a water Sign. These two elements could be an excellent combination when they are working together with their emotions and intelligence to accomplish tasks. Scorpio has a strategy, and can assist Gemini take a step back and understand how to prepare battles before getting into them. Gemini helps Scorpio to relax and let go when their efforts are not successful. Scorpio is often manipulative emotionally and too much water can dampen Gemini's enthusiasm. However, too much Air can agitate the Water and cause difficult sailing for the relationship. Gemini and Scorpio need to work together rather than trying to work in a stalemate to keep their balance.

Gemini is an mutable Sign Gemini is a Mutable Sign, while Scorpio is a fixed Sign. Gemini permits Scorpio the freedom to experience things solely for the pleasure instead of always having an agenda. Scorpio may lead Gemini to a more stable and complete approach to things, rather than bouncing around with no intention of doing any task. Both are committed and attached to one another, and when they understand that they can share the benefits of a satisfying relationship, Gemini providing the reasoning and brain power, and Scorpio as the intense, emotional leader, they will accomplish much in a group.

The most appealing aspect of the friendship between Gemini and Scorpio is their strength that they possess when working together. They are able to champion whatever cause they like and accomplish every goal. Both of them are winners and they'll not quit, creating one-of-a-kind relationship that doesn't settle for less than the highest.

Cancer and Scorpio

In the event that Cancer and Scorpio create a bond two signs that have immense depth come together. Such signs typically are well-matched, with each person's strengths and weaknesses balancing one another. They have a great connection to one another When their thoughts and desires collide together, the temperature of the room is likely to increase! Cancer Scorpio and Scorpio have lots in common that keeps their bond solid.

Cancer and Scorpio are both happy to spend time in a cozy space: Cancer wants comfort, and Scorpio seeks strength. Both signs focus on resources and goods which include bonds, stocks and inheritances. Both are passionate and deeply emotional about every aspect of their lives. They are a perfect match since Cancer Scorpio and Scorpio have a common concern about family and home life and have a strong dedication to the family unit.

Cancer is controlled by the Moon and Scorpio is of the ruling planets Mars along with Pluto. The combination is extremely intense due to the influence of Pluto and influence, however it's a healthy balanced masculine and feminine energy. The two friends that are the foundation for the majority of relationships. The Moon's loving love and Mars's passion. It is believed that the Moon and Mars are compatible The Moon is about rebirth and growth, and Mars is about passion which can be used in creating a deeper friendship and more significant. Scorpio is intense and Cancer is influenced by this. In its turn, Scorpio enjoys the admiration associated with Moon-ruled Cancer.

Cancer Scorpio and Scorpio are both Scorpio and Cancer are both Water Signs. Both are deep signs that, unlike the ocean, you will not really see to the depths. Scorpio as well as Cancer emotionally pull further and deeper into themselves, only to suddenly they roar back with terrifying force. Cancer as well as Scorpio are extremely committed to each other as a result of their common need for emotional and family security. While Cancer is focused on family and the home, Scorpio is more focused on the deeper motives that lie beneath the surface. Scorpio is able to show Cancer more than the top, while Cancer can help Scorpio not to be scared of their emotional impulses. In addition, Scorpio appreciates the Cancerian practicality and Cancer loves Scorpio's egocentricitythis proves that Scorpio truly needs the friendship of its friends.

Cancer is an Cardinal Sign, and Scorpio is an enduring sign. When they reach a common purpose, it can be achieved through their efforts. But, if their viewpoints diverge, beware! Cancer is the first to initiate arguments, and Scorpio is the last to conclude the argument. It is often the case that Cancer will prevail and become the more leading of the two however that's not always the case. Sometimes Scorpio isn't even willing to disagree, even though they may appear to surrender. Both friends are not afraid to use manipulative tactics to get their revenge. It's crucial for them to debate what is important to them both, so they can find a fair agreement. When Scorpio and Cancer are able to trust each other and believe in one another they can accomplish nearly anything with their fervor. The bond will not last in the event that the two are unable to overcome their opinions and stubborn side.

The greatest benefit of the Cancer-Scorpio relationship is their shared emotional energy and the need to be secure. When Cancer recognizes that Scorpio is here for the long haul and the relationship is healthy and nurturing and thriving, the two will be able to flourish together. Their shared determination creates a one of the strongest friendships and determination.

Leo and Scorpio

In the event that Leo and Scorpio make a connection They often form an energetic and powerful pair.

They know each other's requirements very well. Scorpio requires respect and appreciated, while Leo desires to be loved and appreciated. Both are extremely loyaland are often devoted to each other. Both of them are able help each other out and also appreciate the strengths of each other.

Leo loves luxury and comfort and often performs things that are extravagant. Leo is often flamboyant and Scorpio is a fan of that. Scorpio is happy to offer Leo the kind of audience they desire so long as there's the same level of respect in their relationships. Leo shines more intensely and brighter, becoming a model of luxury and elegance. Scorpio is happy to be relieved of the pressure to shine however, they will prefer to be in control of the basics. Since both Signs are determined, they have to come to terms with and respect one another.

Leo is controlled by Leo is ruled by the Sun Leo is ruled by the Sun, while Scorpio is controlled by Planets Mars as well as Pluto. The Sun is all about ego and self-esteem, and emits warmth and energy. Leo certainly radiates this kind of enthusiasm and energy. Mars is all about fighting, battle, and war and Pluto is the one who influences Scorpio's inner thoughts. The ruling planet is Scorpio's House of Sex, Pluto is a major influencer of the concept of rebirth and regeneration which is a common aspect of Scorpio's life. Together, this abundance of male energy is what makes Leo and Scorpio can sooth their differences and support each other. The Sun symbolizes life, while Mars and Pluto symbolize ambition and the unconscious. so long as they're mindful of their interactions their relationship is a powerful and ambitious one.

Leo is an Earth Sign and Scorpio is an Water Sign. Leo is a social person and freedom of speech, while Scorpio is a bouncy and viscous personality. Both signs seek to be leaders in various ways, and this shared desire could cause frustration. As with the Elements that affect the two, they're in a position to destroy each other. Sometimes, their relationship might be unbalanced. But, they will recognize that their small disagreements are not of any real importance, and as they are able to put aside their personal egos and let friendship take precedence and their disagreements to be dealt with.

Scorpio as well as Leo can be considered Fixed Signs as well. Both are stubborn, opinionated and resist changes. Both of them are prone to persevere when they are working towards their objectives. If they've got a plan that they stick to, they'll stay with it until they achieve what they desire. They are generally skeptical of change and prefer life to be steady and stable. If they are unable to agree regarding the same subject it could result in them being fighting for dominance that never ends. Scorpio will not change their minds since they consider it an act of weakness and Leo might think of Scorpio as being too tolerant. If they can see that they're both on the same page in the bigger world It's much easier to stay friendly and effective.

The most appealing feature of the Leo-Scorpio relationship is their commitment to one another and the various activities in which they take part. Both Signs possess extremely powerful yet strategically different personality traits. They are considered strong partners by many and their shared dedication to achieving their goals creates an incredibly strong bond.

Virgo and Scorpio

If Virgo and Scorpio make a connection It's a union between two signs that are different from the Zodiac. It is likely to confer the relationship with a strong connection to the karmic realm. The Virgo-Scorpio relationship is built on loyalty and strong bonds. The majority of the time, this couple tends to be quiet and aren't inclined to join a crowd at dances or parties However, when they are together, they can create a very satisfying collaboration.

Virgo and Scorpio are both averse to working together towards acquisitions: Virgo wants order, and Scorpio is in search of power. Both signs are focused on wealth and assets which includes inheritances and real estate. Virgo is more focused on serving to others. Scorpio is more about the collective, which is why this couple is extremely service-oriented and well-known for their reliability giving a helping hand to friends or the community. In addition, Virgo can be shy and reserved, whereas Scorpio is more transparent. Because of their different personalities each sign can develop and benefit from one another when they agree to be honest with each other.

Virgo is the sign of Mercury and Scorpio is controlled by Mars as well as Pluto. The combination is extremely intense because of the influence of Pluto. Two signs that are in sync create the fundamental basis of human relations, Mercury's communication, and Mars"passion. Mercury and Mars are compatible; Mercury is about the conscious mind, while Mars is all about passion. Scorpio is intense and smoldering and Virgo is drawn by this passion. It is in turn, Scorpio is a fan of the devotion and practicality that is a hallmark of Virgo.

Virgo has been identified as one of the Earth Sign, and Scorpio is an Water Sign. Scorpio is a deep sign. It's an ocean and any disturbance could result in a massive storm! Scorpio gets emotionally involved and, when the pressure gets too intense and the pressure becomes too much, it explodes. Virgo and Scorpio's shared desire for emotional security creates an intense bond between them. While Virgo is simple, with everything laid out in the open, Scorpio is more focused on the subtle nuances of life. Scorpio is able to demonstrate Virgo more than just the physical surface and Virgo is keen enough to be able to discern the subtle conversations. Virgo is able to teach Scorpio to recognize that the facts or figures are often very literal and are often ignored as if they were facts. Scorpio likes the practicality of Virgo and Virgo loves Scorpio's love to them, which proves that they're appreciated.

Virgo is a mutable Sign while Scorpio is a fixed Sign. When they share a common goal, nothing gets between them. If the views of these group members diverge, Virgo is adaptable enough to make a change and avoid allowing a disagreement to occur. Scorpio is often able to find its own way because of an uncompromising streak. It is essential for acquaintances to discuss what's most important to them, so they can play the same roles. This isn't a friendship filled by conflict. The two of them would rather work together instead of fighting.

The greatest benefit of the friendship between Scorpio and Virgo is their strong teamwork when they can agree about their objectives. If Scorpio recognizes that Virgo can be a resource and an equalizing influence in their lives and their relationship, it can flourish. A common determination and a sense of organization make the friendship a formidable power.

Libra and Scorpio

If Libra and Scorpio create a bond It can be a rewarding and stimulating both mentally as well as emotionally. Libra's balanced energy can help counter Scorpio's aloof nature. If they can combine the exceptional interpersonal skills of Libra along with Scorpio's drive and determination They can achieve amazing new heights. Scorpio is more focused than Libra and Libra is able to get the ball moving in the direction that both of them would like to go. Libra and Scorpio are unwavering in their commitment to each other.

This is a focus-driven friendship. It is emotionally and intellectually oriented which makes the bond complex and deep. Scorpio is more patient, however it is also more shrewd than Libra. However, they are companions love taking risks. This is not a boring duo! Libra and Scorpio can have plenty of fun and can be very charming. At times, they may have difficult times understanding each other due to the fact that Libra is very open and upfront and open, whereas Scorpio is more obscure. Both of them must meet often and agree on common guidelines and the boundaries.

Libra has been ruled by Planet Venus, and Scorpio is ruled by two planets Mars as well as Pluto. Libra's ability for communication and love for love and beauty offset the tension that could be caused by the private and emotionally insecure Scorpio. Mars symbolizes passion, therefore Scorpio's energy is a catalyst for an exciting and lively time spent together. Both will not want to fight; Libra doesn't enjoy conflict And Scorpio is likely to pursue revenge in secret. It's usually Libra who initiates an end to war and then comes up with solution. Pluto brings a ferocious edge to this energetic.

Libra is an air Sign as is Scorpio is a water Sign. Both of them can make an excellent combination if they cooperate by using their willpower and intelligence to achieve goals. Scorpio is a strategist , and can assist Libra slow down and understand how to evaluate the waters before taking a plunge. Libra helps Scorpio to be calm and reduce their expenses when they fail. Yet, Scorpio can be emotionally manipulative, with too much water can dampen the

Libran's enthusiasm. However the excess of Air can throw water in the Water and cause Scorpio insane. Libra and Scorpio should plan and work together instead of coming on their own plans to keep the sense of balance they share.

Libra is an Cardinal Sign, while Scorpio is Fixed Sign. Libra introduces a fresh perspective for the relationship, and Scorpio retains the relationship. Both require a lot of dedication and concentration from their companions. Scorpio is able to guide Libra to stabilize and finish things instead of hopping between ideas and another without finishing any task. Each is loyal committed to one another, and when they understand the other, they can have and enjoy a fulfilling friendship. Libra being the one with the rational and brain power as well as Scorpio as the fiery emotional force.

The most appealing aspect of the Libra-Scorpio partnership is the strength they can achieve when they work together. They are able to achieve a lot together. They're both winners and they'll never ever give up, resulting in an enduring friendship that will take into consideration the business.

Scorpio and Scorpio

If two Scorpions establish an alliance and bond, they form an intense and passionate couple. They both are in love with each other The relationship may grow faster than the average. The interactions between them are intense but at the same time, and to the opposite end, disagreements will also be extremely powerful. The friendship could be the best experience of the world, or be the demise of the parties in the relationship.

The fusion of two Scorpions could unleash the best of bothof them, using their intuitive and emotional natures to become the best and most trusted friends you can have. The determination and strength can keep them fighting the battle for each other. So long as they are committed to their alliance, no external forces will be able to interfere. Both of these powerful signs are able to be a good match in the event that they can learn the best way to harness their power effectively this isn't an easy task for Scorpio.

Scorpio is under the control of Scorpio is ruled by the Planets Mars as well as Pluto. Mars is the old God of War Always advancing with passion, aggression and brave. Pluto is higher in Octave than Mars and has the destruction, power and rebirth aspects of the Scorpio-Scorpio relationship. The two planets enable the Scorpion to rebound after the loss of a loved one. Lucky for the Scorpion since their intense emotions increase the importance and the loss of everything.

Scorpio is an Water Sign, thus their initial reaction to any event is an intense emotional reaction. The most valuable thing for the Scorpio is to manage the violent or vindictive aspect of their personalities and to revel in the most extreme highs and swiftly forget about the downs. Get out there and tell us what you truly would like to say! If you keep your emotions secret, they can take away the framework that keeps you and your partner together so well. Since you're two of the same, jealousy could cause problems. Be strong, courageous Scorpio and conquer obstacles in a group!

Scorpio is fixed Sign. Two Fixed Signs in tandem may take turns filling the other's cups with new ideas. Together you accomplish your goals! This is an excellent mix for working partners and personal relationships. Together, you've got the most brilliant ideas for investing and sharing resources. Scorpio is sure to research deeply before moving forward to the next amazing idea. You'll have no problem getting a project completed if both of you have committed to the project's completion.

The most appealing aspect of the Scorpio-Scorpio relationship is the intense admiration these friends feel. You're very focused, and your common strength is what makes you an unbeatable duo! Utter commitment ensures that your friendship will last for a long period of time.

Sagittarius and Scorpio

If Scorpio and Sagittarius make a connection and they form a bond, they must be patient and careful not to leap into the action. The patience they show will pay off! Sagittarius thrives on the variety, newness and optimism. Scorpio appreciates the interactions that strengthen the pair's emotional bonds. At the beginning of their friendship, Sagittarius may feel somewhat restricted by Scorpio's demands However, If Scorpio manages to manage their emotions the pair could have a an intense and thrilling friendship.

Scorpio and Sagittarius both have an enlightening perspective on life that is evocative and explorative. They enjoy sharing adventures. Sagittarius might feel Scorpio to be rigid and rigid. Scorpio may feel that Sagittarius can be sometimes too hotheaded. Together , they love sharing information and exploring new locations. Their bond is never ending.

Scorpio is controlled by Pluto and Mars The Scorpions are ruled by Mars and Pluto. Sagittarius is the ruling planet of Jupiter. Mars is known as the God of War and is the one who opens the door for Scorpio's strong, brave character. Mars when paired with Pluto is a symbol of revival and renewal. Jupiter is focused on the philosophy of higher learning expansion, optimism, luck, and travel. The combination of masculine energy and growth is what makes them admire and support each other.

Scorpio is one of the Water Sign, and Sagittarius is the Fire Sign. Sagittarius creates projects on the basis of pure enthusiasm and spontaneity While

Scorpio's motives are more subtle. They may struggle to figure out what inspires each other. source of inspiration. If they both are in agreement that friendship is essential, their love and respect for each other will be the most valuable help.

Scorpio is a fixed Sign The Scorpion is a Fixed Sign. Sagittarius is Mutable Sign. Both signs are at the forefront of multiple projects, but only with the help of Scorpio the tasks will be accomplished. But, Sagittarius likes to move from project to project at the speed of light. It's not difficult for Sagittarius to observe and appreciate Scorpio's efforts since Sagittarius is more observant. Scorpion is more obstinate and holds high standards. However, Scorpio needs to give Sagittarius the liberty to explore their own world and desires. Scorpio can help Sagittarius' ideas come into the point of realization, even when Sagittarius has abandoned their interests and moved on. Sagittarius could teach Scorpio that flexibility is often more effective than a firm determination.

The most appealing aspect of the Scorpio-Sagittarius bond is the stability and security they offer one another. They form a harmonious couple once they are able to see the world through their own perspectives and are open with each their fellows. If they can discuss and appreciate their differences, it will be a strong bond.

Capricorn and Scorpio

If Scorpio and Capricorn create a bond and they help each other grow as individuals and learn the importance of a love relationship. Reticence, fear and distrust of others can diminish the initial effect of this relationship. It takes time for the two to be open to one another and to feel at ease as a couple. Once they've developed the ability to trust, communicate and love one another and their relationship will be strong and secure.

Scorpio as well as Capricorn have plenty to learn from each other and many things to learn with each other. Scorpio is able to control their fiery emotions thanks to Capricorn's dependable and steady behavior. But, this attitude could be a problem for Scorpio who might become frustrated by Capricorn's lack of emotional depth. Capricorn is able to learn to look deeper within their own lives and in all areas of their lives from their more passionate friend. Both signs share a passion for committing to a project.

Scorpio is controlled by the planets Mars and Pluto The planets Mars and Pluto rule Scorpio, while Capricorn has been ruled by Planet Saturn. Mars and Pluto represent courage, aggression sexual energy, renewal and rebirth. Saturn imparts the most important lessons of life, such as hard work, determination, ambition, and responsibility. Both Signs are a perfect combination to create an unstoppable union bonded by the ferocity of Scorpio and Capricorn's impulsive actions. This is a dynamic couple.

Scorpio is an Water Sign, and Capricorn is an Earth Sign. The Earth is associated with things of the material world and with possessions. This is an ideal equilibrium for the Water element, which is known to adopt the shape of an event by way of an emotional response. If flexibility and stability are the norm for Capricorn and Scorpio and Scorpio, respectively, they can both effectively impart their wisdom and talents with their companions.

Scorpio is an Fixed Sign, and Capricorn is an astrological sign that is

Cardinal. Capricorn typically initiates new and beneficial initiatives for themselves and their surroundings. Scorpio is usually happy to develop ideas of their friend however, they will also want to add their own ideas. It is advisable for Capricorn to take a moment to listen, then open the communications channels as wide as is possible to their companion. Both signs are resistant, which could cause conflict. Additionally, Scorpio is much more emotionally invested in their relationship that Capricorn. Sea Goat, and perhaps more so than Capricorn can handle. Both of them must acknowledge this and accept their relationship is fortunate.

The most appealing aspect of the friendship between Scorpio and Capricorn is their commitment to sharing ideas as well as their dedication to each other. They are able to learn from each other different ways of seeing.

Aquarius and Scorpio

If Scorpio and Aquarius make a connection that is a mix of diverse needs and different views. Scorpio has a strong emotional sensitivity that they deal with their daily lives. Aquarius has an unique and idealistic view of the world. While Scorpio might be more reserved and prefers to work on their own, Aquarius enjoys socializing with other people. It may seem like they share some common interests, but they are both capable of a strong willpower. If they can commit this effort to accomplish a purpose, they are certain of having fun and success.

They both Scorpio and Aquarius are both challenging and opinionated. They are the type of people who like things in according to their preferences without question. Scorpio is a shrewd, discerning soul who digs deep into the significance of the things. Aquarius can be modern, and does not like attention to detail. Scorpio is likely to find Aquarius thrilling, however, they might be frustrated when trying to break into the revolutionary's mind. Aquarius isn't awed by the stinging Scorpion or the level of attention they demand however, they will appreciate the energy Scorpio can provide as a wonderful source of help.

Scorpio is and is ruled by Planets Mars as well as Pluto as well as Aquarius is controlled by Saturn and Uranus. Mars is a wild aggressive, belligerent, and courageous masculine energy and Pluto stimulates these energies and provides a rebirthing cycle-like character. Saturn is an energy that is cool and contained and Uranus is all about everything unique and different. Mars is emotional, reacting and not taking things into consideration; that is the character of Scorpio. It is for Aquarius, Saturn is about determination and hard work to accomplish goals. Uranus influences thinking ahead. Scorpio can teach Aquarius about the way to live that is based on emotions and how to look deeper than the layer of the surface. Aquarius can help Scorpio to remain more detached to be detached from uncontrollable circumstances and reconsider their objectives if they're not on the right track.

Scorpio is one of the Water Sign, and Aquarius is an Air Sign. Aquarius goes about life with an unrelenting, creative exploration, whereas Scorpio is more focused. Scorpio is focused and Aquarius seeks out the thrilling. Both of them could have a difficult time finding out where the other's opinions originate. The two could get into a fight in the event that Scorpio is too dominant or Aquarius is too cool and smug and refuses to give Scorpio assurance. Both partners must learn that they perceive the world differently and they ought to be happy and be jolly about their differences.

Scorpio as well as Aquarius Both are Fixed signs. Both of them can be stubborn, solitary and uncompromising. Both partners tend to persevere when working towards the goal. If they've got a plan and stick to it, they'll do so until they're rewarded for their efforts. When they've made their minds to achieve things together, they'll not let up on maintaining the relationship. If they disagree on a particular idea it could be they are they are the Scorpion will be the determined and more rigid companion. If both of them believe in the importance of their relationship They will be in a position to overcome any differences they encounter.

The most appealing aspect of the Scorpio-Aquarius partnership is the potential for victory and glory through their synergy. Both Signs are extremely strong personalities, which means neither will be able to overpower each one. If they can work the differences and join together and be able to agree on their own individuality and preferences, the results of this relationship can be delicious.

Pisces and Scorpio

If Scorpio and Pisces create a bond They enjoy a great connection. Both signs are associated with the same element, water and are able to understand the other. Scorpio is extremely in-depth and secretive, and is often getting caught up in their own plans, whereas Pisces is idealistic and is looking at the nuances of an event. But, Pisces also has a tendency to stay in their own world and accept Scorpio as being mysterious and withdrawing at times.

Both signs are observant and are aware of humanity's subtlenuances of interactions. Scorpio can assist Pisces achieve their dreams and goals in order to transform thoughts into reality. The Scorpion can provide a solid base that the relationship can be built around, while the more fleeting and sensitive Fish is bound to the web of Scorpio. As a result, Pisces offers gentleness, compassion and kindness that Scorpio loves and admires. Scorpio is attracted by certain things that make life comfortable and in intense emotional dramas. It often is not able to grasp the simple, generous nature of Pisces. Their goals for the long-term are not the same. When they learn to overcome the differences and make it an extremely rewarding friendship.

Scorpio is the astrological signification of its own Planets Mars as well as Pluto Scorpio is ruled by Pluto and Mars, while Pisces is controlled by Jupiter and Neptune. Mars is considered to be the oldest God of War and Scorpio is a testimony to its bold, courageous bold and sometimes aggressive influence. When paired with Pluto the planet of fire turns cyclical and signifies the rebirth of life and the beginning of new ones. Scorpio can withstand an enormous amount of pressure and bounce back. But the Scorpion also has the ability to unleash the energy with a vengeance! Pisces is also rulered by Jupiter. It is a symbol of expansion, philosophy and exaggerations. The Neptunian influence can give Pisces an aura of dreaminess and a love of media and popular culture. This enchanting energy soothes Scorpio's sharp edges. It is the nature that this planet combination provides a mutually beneficial relationship that is soaked in passion and intrigue, and infused with a true celestial connection. But, Scorpio must be careful not to over-stress the floating Fish because

Pisces is likely to be overwhelmed by the pressure of too many demands.

Scorpio as well as Pisces are both Pisces and Scorpio are both Water Signs. They are generally very compatible because Water can be a real physical thing and both are aware of this. Pisces is designed to bring people together and when they join together with Scorpio's enthrallement and perseverance, there's no greater connection. Furthermore, Scorpio has an absolutist conception of life that everything is either gold or tarnished. Pisces is a good sign to allow for a variety of possibilities instead of focusing on a single thing. Scorpio might get tired of Pisces instability and Pisces might believe that Scorpio is insular and unresponsive to their requirements. It's relatively simple for them to reach the right balance.

Scorpio is a Fixed Sign while Pisces is a mutable sign. Scorpio is usually focused on a single task at a given time, but Pisces prefers to shift between projects as the mood takes them. Pisces is a natural part of Scorpio's hobbies and projects. Then, Scorpio must allow Pisces the ability to indulge in their own passions. Pisces may prove to Scorpio that flexibility is often more effective than a rigid determination and that compromises without effort can be rewarded. Scorpio and Pisces are a good match and draw from the other's energy and are a good match in business and friendship.

The greatest benefit of the relationship between Scorpio and Pisces is the similarity in their emotional lives. They complement and complement each other extremely well. The total commitment and empathy these two signs indicate in friendship is what keeps the bonds of friendship strong and last between Scorpion and the Fish.

Chapter 5: Scorpio Woman

Scorpio Woman Profile

Scorpio sign is controlled by Pluto and is the 8th zodiac sign. It's a water sign which is fixed, meaning that the woman is quiet emotionally, deep and intimate. The words mystery and suspense are the two of the words that describe the Scorpio woman once you meet her. The Scorpio woman has lots of personality and is often filled with unexpected events. She is determined and successful. She is also determined. She will strive to accomplish the goals she has set for herself as fast and efficiently as is possible. She is a faithful person who is a loving and supportive person to be with. If she is aware of people who are struggling, she will help the person as best as she can. She will also assist in solving the problems of her friends by utilizing her wit and insight.

In a love affair that is committed she is committed and loyal. She is beautiful and can attract every man she wishes. She is hardworking and her drive allows her to achieve what she desires in the modern world of hurried living. She is a great colleague, offering support to every aspect of her work. She is strong and has a dualistic character. Scorpions possessing a powerful will power adhere to their beliefs with fervour and this is due to the water aspect that produces high pressure similar to deep-water or ice. This is the reason she is so elusive and intuitive. She is also charismatic and awe-inspiring.

Because scorpions are very extremely passionate and intense, they may become obsessed by the work she is doing, which is the reason why many people who have this sign have a lot of success. In this way, they are able to dream of a larger ambition and may attain it just like the snooping snake searching to catch its quarry. However , the woman with this type of attitude tends to be elusive or possessive, resentful, and jealous. They can also be suspicious and stubborn. If she is a victim, she will be in danger of being a disaster and she will never forget the harm or humiliation she has caused her.

Scorpio Woman

A woman born under the sign of the scorpio never wins an Scorpio female. It requires a man who understands exactly what he is looking for to stand his own against the woman born in this sign. Scorpio woman is extremely emotional, extremely affectionate and extremely demanding. She's not interested in the pleasure of a flirt or sleeping arrangement. She also doesn't believe in the concept of sharing. Anyone who believes it's not required to sign a contract just because he's in a relationship with women would be wise to stay clear of a relationship with an Scorpio female. She's a big believer in treaties with irrevocable clauses and lots fine print that spells out exactly what you aren't allowed to do.

How can she get out of being so ostracized and jealous? Because she's a stunning captivating, captivating, irresistible lady. She is a joy to be around, when she is in her bedroom and and entertaining when she is in her living space. She has an intriguing aura of mystery. She is able to drive men to the edge of despair, and then with a single gesture bring her back to apex of happiness. There's no room for compromise with this flamboyant female. If you were a woman of the zodiac, you could come up with a compromise on who is entitled and who has been wronged. This is not the case with her. You must be willing to compromise and take the best deal of the bargain, or accept living in the midst of an ongoing earthquake.

Love is a major factor for Her, she will generate enough attraction to attract men of all kinds. If the man she is interested in is specialto her, she's willing to take on the role of the aggressor. The dynamo of her is set to go off when her amazing senses inform her that this guy is one she will be content with. Her instincts are never wrong. She has the ability to discover the hidden mysteries in human behavior. She also can be able to see into men's sexual fantasies and through her imaginative methods, keep him on the edge.

Scorpio is an element of water, and , like all Water significations (Cancer, Scorpio, Pisces) Scorpio is extremely vulnerable to the thoughts of other people. The greatest desire of hers is for a closeand passionate relationship. In a relationship, she can't tolerate casualness or coldness or the feeling that she is being ignored. When she is in love, she is the most vulnerable because someone can hurt her without realizing that it has happened. A woman may forgive and forget, but when a Scorpio victimized,, she will always fight at the other side. If she has to, she will take out her anger.

In spite of the stories about Scorpio's passionate, willful nature, she's an unwavering lover to the person she selects to be her own. It is a sign that has a certain permanence and she is blessed with an inexhaustible capacity to be loyal. One could not ask for an ally more fierce than her. If a Scorpio woman is in love with you she will protect and defend you to the end of time. She demands constancy. What she provides is loyalty. She's possessive and most men who have the Scorpio woman within their lives will admit that they'd love to be controlled by her.

Chapter 6: Scorpioman

Scorpio Man Profile

The traits that are exhibited by the Scorpio man are unlike any other. It often occurs that certain characteristics observed in those born under various zodiac signs are a little similar however the Scorpio man is completely distinct in his character. The major part of his character and life is controlled by the desire to be passionate. The desire to live a life that is modern and work, love, and so on. is the primary reason for the majority of his actions. Passion is what drives him to take decisions that may be against any logic. Because of the force of his passion, everything about him is affected in some way by this. The relationships he has with his loved ones aren't exempt. The man must feel a rush of passion that is fueled by emotions and intense desires for a girl, or he'll not be attracted. A male who is a Scorpio does not believe in patience or low-key conversations, his instincts will determine if the attraction to a girl is authentic.

Many women find this type of passion attractive for this Scorpio man, however, it is important to recognize that this passion is an enigma with two sides. He may be a passionate love at the moment, but this could result in obsessiveness or jealousy. tomorrow. This is due to the fact that both negative and positive emotions are driven by passion and therefore the actions and reactions tend to be extreme. Certain of these negative characteristics are further accentuated by a stubborn mindset. It's extremely difficult and virtually impossible for the Scorpio man to believe that he could be incorrect. Therefore, certain aspects of their personality require patience from their love partners. In reality, if one wants to enter into a loving relationship with an Scorpio man, then she'll need to be patient with many things. This is just one of the negative aspects , however it is well-known that Scorpios are great companions. If they trust someone they will stick by their loved ones no matter the consequences.

Another thing to bear in mind when it comes to the Scorpio male is that she prefers to be dominant and controlling position regardless of the situation he's in. This means that they like to be the boss in the office and at home. This could not be an issue as the need to be dominant can also motivate him to strive to be the best in all initiatives he takes part in the present. He is a very motivated person with a desire to succeed in life, as well as in the love arena. This makes him want to scrub things that influence his behavior in a manner which could hinder his chances of achievement. It's almost impossible for anyone born with this type of personality to ever think about giving up on what they are totally focused on. In the context of the situation, this trait could be either a positive thing or a disadvantage.

Scorpio Man

Scorpions are extremely passionate and driven by nature striving for the highest standard in everything they put their minds to. With the determination and persistence in addition, this creates competitive men with the best chance of being successful and reaching their objectives. Similar to that it is possible to dismiss those things that could be hindering him or hindering him from reaching his goals. Due to his intense love for the things and people that he enjoys, it spills over into the other areas of the way he lives. If he is passionate for something or anyone, it will manifest in every word he speaks and act. The Scorpion man is caught up in the excitement in the present. The emotions are in full force or they are not there even. Talking about nothing and being patient doesn't suffice with the Scorpio. He'll follow his intuition and with fervor, wherever it takes him.

Women can sense in him an energy that is magnetic and sexuality is only one aspect of this magnetic force. He exudes a sense of mystery and strength and a frightful and unpredictable presence. One reason Scorpio is so infamously bad image is that his flaws manifest more clearly in his relationships than any other part of his life. No other thing can bring out what extremes in his character is exposed as sexual sex.

He's got so much enthusiasm and energy that you'll be able to seduce the guy, even if it's what you're looking for. The trickier part is to build a relationship with him. It's not because the man doesn't desire to be in a relationship, but because it's actually precisely what he would need. He is a very sensitive person who is easily wounded and often feels unfulfilled and lonely. The issue with jealousies is unresolved angers can be very difficult to deal with. He has the least defensible defenses of the zodiac. The one thing he'll never let you know is his vulnerability. He will not allow women to rule him. If he wants to that, he is able to let a woman hang in his tether for until he is satisfied with her. If he decides to let her go however brutal the breakup may be it will be a surprise when she displays any anger. He's the only person who is entitled to take revenge.

When it comes to love, He always has a clear idea of the price of what he desires until the very last decimal. If the price is too expensive, economically, emotionally or otherwise, he'll not negotiate. He'll just go away. The Scorpio man is sly and difficult to comprehend even though he is often pleasant, friendly and easygoing. What you can see from the outside is what he would like you to observe. However, even when he's very friendly, and it is however, there's an underlying risk to this guy.

He knows the attractiveness he has to women and takes advantage of it. In his method of making women love him, He plans his actions carefully and isn't wasting time, but never appearing impatient. He's direct and powerful and there aren't many women that can resist his simple sexual attraction. He is able to bring out the complete sexuality potential of every woman with whom he has an intense relationship. One of the aspects that make him truly distinctive as a partner is that he is able to comprehend the needs of women and as long as he's not afraid will do his best to meet the needs of his partner. The vivacious, energetic male can be quite a bit to bear, but the Scorpio man can make a woman feel like she's the most attractive woman she could be.

Chapter 7: Scorpio Attraction

How to attract Scorpio

Scorpios are known for their unpredictable nature. However, there are some general guidelines that could be a useful guide. Pay attention to the Scorpio with a keen ear and complete concentration. It's impossible to fake it. Scorpios will always detect the difference between lying and deceit and it will be the end of the story before there's any beginning. Remember an overriding Scorpio trait: curiosity. Never inform the Scorpio that something happened , without providing the reason or how. If you don't include that information then you'll be regarded as either boring or superficial. The two types don't get along when it comes to people born in this category.

They love all sorts of entertainment, especially water activities. If you're the kind of person who would like a relaxing time at the beach or to take a trip on a fishing vessel or to go for a water ski instruction, you and Scorpio are likely to have a lot in common. Scorpios like events, social gatherings including charity events, charity bazaars, and other places to be with people who are successful. If you are involved in an dispute (and you shouldn't do that with any person that is born with this sign) be sure to behave in a respectful manner. Scorpios are serious, proud and do not believe that any of their views shouldn't be questioned even if they are funny.

Aries and Scorpio

At first, the attraction to Scorpio is intense. In terms of sexuality, Aries is more imaginative and more open to experiments However, Scorpio's burning desires show a perfect match. The dangers are elsewhere however. Both are self-centered and are determined to take the right decisions. There's a fundamental conflict of wills, because Aries is a dominant sign and Scorpio seeks to dominate. Scorpio's aloof and tense nature is not a good fit for open and impulsive Aries. Aries is a free-spirited, outgoing and flirtatious, and this can irritate jealous, possessive Scorpio. Sexual differences can be a hindrance to the relationship.

Taurus and Scorpio

Taurus has the strength and the drive to please Scorpio at night. But how will the two lovers do for the remaining 23 and a half-hours of the day? Both are extremely insecure and jealous. The difference between them is that Taurus would like to own the love of his life, as if it were the value of a piece of art, while Scorpio is looking to acquire emotionally. Although they have a love for money, Scorpio is thrifty and is prone to laziness, while Taurus prefers spending money on comforts. Scorpio is determined, Taurus is obstinate, and both would like to be captains of what could become sinking ship.

Gemini and Scorpio

Scorpio is attracted by Gemini's enthusiasm and the Scorpio's fascinating personality captivates interested Gemini. At times, Gemini is also fascinated by the constant sexual demands of Scorpio. However, Gemini is too volatile and unchanging for fierce Scorpio who demands and expects complete commitment. Unrestful Gemini has a keen desire for independence, whereas Scorpio seeks to be dominant and be a king. Scorpio is essentially a loner; Gemini likes to glitter in social situations. There will be some fun frolics however, all too soon the fun wanes and Gemini begins to look for a way to get out.

Cancer and Scorpio

It can be a lucrative combination. Cancer is the one who plays it safe however there's plenty of combustible material that can ignite from Scorpio's abundance of passions. The heat of the bedroom will help in cooling off the tensions that can develop between two people who are jealous. Scorpio provides strength and protection and that's exactly what insecure, clinging Cancer seeks. It is in turn, Cancer is generous, affectionate, loving, and committed to all the things

Scorpio seeks. They get along as if they were jam and bread.

Leo and Scorpio

Scorpio isn't going to flatter Leo's self-esteem or acknowledge Leo's power. Scorpio is looking to penetrate the erotic mind of a lover. Leo is looking for a grand romance. Tempers and passions are equally powerful in both. A fiery Leo can be extravagant, and loves to live life on a grand scale, while Scorpio dislikes the appearance of other people and inefficiency. There's plenty affection between the two, however both have a fragile limb. Scorpio's jealousy could provide sparks, and once the fire goes off it will be a blast!

Virgo and Scorpio

Restrained Virgo is unable to keep up with the highly agitated Scorpio and isn't sure what this all fuss and angst is about. There's a wonderful connection between the two and a wonderful mix of personalities. Both are dedicated to their family and the security of their finances. Both aren't impulsive or shallow The deep emotions that each has can lead to solid devotion and loyalty. They share so much in common that perhaps Scorpio isn't too concerned that Virgo's desires are more physical than intellectual.

Libra and Scorpio

The unpredictable nature of Scorpio immediately entices Libra who loves collecting interesting people. Scorpio is a perfect match for Libra's need for love-- and even more. Scorpio's jealousy can make a good impression on Libra. However, Libra is a perpetual flirt and Scorpio is extremely sensitive and intimate. Afflicted Scorpio is one who takes love and commitment very seriously. Libra is looking for a partner who can improve its image. The Libran's erratic attitude towards affection will irritate and upset Scorpio. The mingling won't result in anything lasting.

Scorpio and Scorpio

There's plenty of sexual attraction But the temperature of the emotions cannot continue to rise for ever. Two people who look very similar to each one another extremely small. They are both extremely competitive and jealous. They're so intense that any small storm transforms into an engulfing hurricane. Both are brooding, sulky and jealous. Both are engaged in a constant struggle to force each other to surrender control. There's something that has to be sacrificed and if it does it's likely to mean The End.

Sagittarius and Scorpio

Sagittarius's unbridled, free-spirited style. Scorpio is a dominant sign, but it's not able to keep the wild, uncontrollable Sagittarius in a trance for too long. Sagittarius believes that the focus should be on having fun and new adventures. Scorpio seeks security and continuous love. Sagittarius is very open, friendly and casual when it comes to relationships. Scorpio is shy and secretive. They are also very attracted to relationships. Scorpio is looking to keep Sagittarius to be at home, Sagittarius is a wanderer. A relationship without a plan for the future.

Capricorn and Scorpio

All the passions that Scorpio is known for are embraced here. Scorpio's volatile emotions can release their inner-directed, brooding Capricorn and the lively events add spice to a loving emotional connection. Scorpio even enjoys Capricorn's jealousy because this helps Capricorn feel secure. Both share a sense of direction They are committed, ambitious, and committed to their responsibility as a group. Together, they are a good bet for financial achievement. They must have clear sailing.

Aquarius and Scorpio

Scorpio has a lot of emotional demands however Aquarius is a different animal. Aquarius even a romance is just another opportunity to expand its perspectives. Scorpio isn't able to accept Aquarius's independence when it comes to relationships or the casual attitude of Aquarius towards affection. Aquarius is far too detached with too numerous external pursuits to fit the egocentric jealous Scorpio. Scorpio is determined to rule and be irritated by Aquarius's unpredictable moods , and desire for freedom. Scorpio would prefer to remain at home. Aquarius would like to be free to move about. The cycle continues, until the final.

Pisces and Scorpio

Scorpio's strength makes it a great protection against Pisces's lack of clarity. The Pisces's imagination inspires Scorpio's creativeness. Pisces can provide Scorpio the love and respect that it desires and their shared attraction to love creates an elegant romantic ambiance. Pisces's love of the absurd can add a touch of humour to Scorpio's desire and the intense emotional requirements of both signs coincide. The intuitiveness of Pisces and Scorpio's deep sense of sensuality are a perfect match for a closeness. The kind of mating that occurs is lasting.

Chapter 8: All Signns Aspects

Zodiac Signs Elements

Many people look up the meanings of their zodiac signs to gain insight into their own lives and those they live with. The twelve zodiac's astrological signs are divided in four different elements which depend on. This includes water, earth as well as fire and air. All zodiac signs belong to any of the elements, which have unique characteristics for each.

Zodiac Signs - Earth

The initial element that is mentioned is Earth and the signs that fall into it are blessed with many good qualities. Earth people tend to be solid and grounded which makes them hard-working who thrive on growth and progress. One of the signs that are part of this element is Taurus. It is known as the most powerful and stable of all zodiac signs. They are not averse to changes and prefer regularity and a solid base. The other sign is Virgo and is very flexible, analytical and stable. They are the most physical of the Earth Astrological signs and are typically pure in their nature. The final Earth symbol is Capricorn with numerous sides. They are curious about the meaning behind almost everything in their lives and could be a workaholic when someone is not able to with the balance.

Zodiac Signs - Water

Three astrology signs are present that belong to the element Water. The element of water is one of the most emotional four, and can easily be wounded and highly sensitive of other signs. Cancer is among the most well-known signs of Water signs as they can be very supportive and supportive of other people. Next Water sign is Scorpio. They are full of energy and energy, just like an angry river. They are often required to be able to focus for their feelings to stay in control, much like the dams that keep rivers from becoming wild. The final Water sign is the Pisces which is a resemblance to a small stream. The people who have this sign tend to be beautiful and innovative. The Pisces is thought to be to be the most spiritual among the zodiac symbolisms.

Zodiac Signs - Fire

Fire is the Fire element is well-known for its passion as well as passion, anger and. The signs that are part of this element may be fast to anger and extremely impulsive and fast-moving. First, the sign of Aries which is very active and temperamental in specific circumstances. The middle fire sign is Leo. Like the lion who is the symbol of that sign, these signs enjoy being in the spotlight. They can be extremely romantic and are often modest. The final sign is Sagittarius. They are known for being highly introverted and creative. They usually end up becoming poets, artists or musicians looking to make works that have meaning.

Zodiac Signs - Air

The final element is Air which is known for its profound and mysterious nature as well as their deep thinking. Gemini is the most famous of them all. Gemini is the primary symbol and is usually uncertain and unpredictable. Another zodiac symbol is Libra who is famous for keeping an equilibrium across all zodiac signs. They are adamant about fairness and justice and work to maintain the balance. The final Air Signs is Aquarius. They are extremely strong with emotions and are frequently regarded as the most sophisticated thinker.

Aries - Fire Sign

The most important Zodiac Sign is Aries and is the sign of the beginning of various things. Aries people are the first to go and generally have a quick personality. They're typically assertive and single-track focused. This assertive nature can also be stubbornly aggressive when negatively-channeled. If used constructively it's viewed as a leader, and they can achieve the most creative tasks. Their confidence and strength allow them to accomplish things that other signs see as being impossible. Aries usually know what they are looking for and are not shy about letting their desires be recognized. They don't like losing arguments, so they are adamant about compromising. Because of their reliability, honesty and integrity They are excellent people to be around. If a person needs help, they'll stand by them throughout the day and out. People of the Aries are awestruck by the possibilities as well. With their confidence they trust that they'll be successful.

Taurus- Earth Sign

A second sign that is part of the zodiac is Taurus and those from this sign usually make wonderful partners. They do not mind sharing the bad and good aspects of relationships. They will also be accountable for their actions rather than leaving it to others to manage. The persona of Taurus Taurus is open and honest and honest, two traits that allow them to achieve the tasks they need to complete precisely and also have the time to relax. A lot of people are positively influenced by people who are born under this sign. It can inspire people to be consistent and open about their personal concerns. Both female and male Taurus are easily identified through their vivacious appearance and beautiful facial features. The planet Venus governs Taurus and symbolizes romantic love and pursuits of the creative. These traits are the reason for the Taurus romantic and enjoyable side , as well as remarkable balance for its more practical traits.

Gemini - Air Sign

The Gemini people have a variety of talents and interests, which means their attention is divided between a variety of things. It's quite common for them to begin with a task only to be caught up in another thing. This is the kind of thing however that will bring them the results they seek because they are able to accomplish things in a brief period of time much superior to the average person. If confronted with a variety of precise information and data, Gemini is the Gemini can manage everything better than the other. When most sun signs be suffocated by stress and pressure, Gemini is not. Gemini thrives in the face of these pressures, which boosts their energy and enthusiasm. Gemini is controlled by the Twins and enjoys the dualistic nature as the variety that is its nature. Gemini knows that life is complex and isn't afraid of the multitude of opportunities to be attained in a single minute of the day.

Cancer Water Sign

The persona associated with the Cancer sign is deeply rooted in the realm of the home and family. While that's true however, that does not mean that they won't be able to find satisfaction in their work. In fact, Cancer folk are highly creatively accurate in their endeavors. They just take their loved ones' wellbeing the top priority. Because they take the burden of caring for the physical and mental well-being the Cancer also requires assistance in their business and financial aspects. Cancer sufferers are usually nurturing and innate. They are aware of what they would like to achieve in their lives and are able to overcome any obstacles. When they meet someone who has an Cancer personality are usually amazed by their strength and determination; these traits aid them in forming their life's most important values. Both genders of Cancer is recognized through their mature outlook on life, as well as their physical speed of reaction.

Leo - Fire Sign

The lion is the symbol of this symbol, indicating self-esteem, grace and humility. People who are Leos can be wounded by personal insults or insults. But, they're usually compassionate due to their great nature and genuine generosity. They are a kind and compassionate people. Leo personality is well-known for its charisma and, with their convincing smiles, they are able to achieve almost anything they want. They are proud of their appearance, and possess an animal magnetism that can turn heads wherever they go. Of of course, Leos don't rely just on their appearance and charisma; they're blessed with precise creativity and power. In general, they are regarded as natural leaders, Leos are often accused of being arrogant or insecure. However, their perseverance and self-assurance ensures that they achieve their goals. When things don't go as they had planned they will take care of the situation. In social interactions, Leo is a great companion to have because their character will bring joy to someone's life.

Virgo - Earth Sign

Virgos are driven to be precise, perfect and truthful in everything. They are as dedicated on their job as they can to make sure that the job is completed correctly first time around. This is why they expect their colleagues to be as meticulous in their work as they themselves are. Their ability to improve the tiny and vital things that others overlook is a key element in their achievement. Virgos are well-known for their promises, and people rely on them to ensure that things are done right the first time. They know that they can trust Virgos and for this reason, they will seek a the services of a Virgo to complete complex and/or significant projects. The Virgo sign is considered to be one of the most practical zodiac signs. They aren't afraid of having fun like other zodiac signs, but they are more at ease when they are able to combine productive and leisure time together. Virgos are often advised to be more relaxed; however in the overall perspective most people appreciate the Virgos their ability to complete tasks without fuss.

Libra - Air Sign

People who are born with Libra are those who Libra sign are committed to truth, equality and fairness. Therefore, it's not unusual to come across the Libra working as an arbitrator to offer advice and provide an accurate opinion on a range of topics. Libras have the ability to communicate with a quiet style that allows others to readily be in agreement with them. People look at Libras' balanced attitude with admiration. The Libra woman and man want harmony in their daily lives and, as a result they possess a distinct artistic sense that they bring to their work and home lives. The Libra seeks balance and harmony within themselves. This usually happens by enlisting the help of a companion who will help the Libra their true beauty. When it comes to friendships Libras tend to be best acquaintances with people who share the same respect for them of all the wonderful things in their lives.

Scorpio - Water Sign

The Scorpio male and female are renowned for their individual magnetism and their true intensity. The Scorpio sign is characterized by a strong inner strength that, if properly developed, can give them the ability to transform the negative situation into something constructive and precise. They are able to transform their negative energy into something positive. The sign of the zodiac can sense they're constantly dealing with difficult circumstances. However, they can transform these difficulties into strengths which boost confidence and strength in their. Scorpio has been compared with that mythical Phoenix bird that is reborn from the ashes, and is more beautiful in appearance and strength than the one before. Scorpios are active and energetic; with their determination, intelligence, and convincing character, they're frequently recognized as leaders or powerful posts. They are frequently admired and recognized for their eyes that are intense and swift body movement.

Sagittarius - Fire Sign

One of the most important characteristics of the Sagittarius persona is their need to be always involved in life and remain active. Sagittarius are avid travelers and change jobs regularly and engage in a myriad of activities at different times and then deciding to focus on something different. They shouldn't be thought of as a shrewd or naive. Instead it should be taken as a positive indication of their incredible energy and an intelligent mind that is able to handle every kind of issue. If the

Sagittarius is able to identify something that is essential and true they'll devote their energy and focus on this thing. It's the Sagittarius sign is known for their enthusiasm and unstoppable energy, allowing them to accomplish and achieve a variety of things.

Capricorn - Earth Sign

The female and male Capricorn personality is usually smarter and educated than those around them. They're also clever and smart enough to feel conceited about it. This sign's personality is evident with solid determination. The goat represents the Capricorn that is thought of as being a tough animal with great strength. The Capricorn personality is like the mountain goat that does not go straight to the top , but rather traverses difficult paths until it reaches the highest point. A Capricorn will not always get immediate satisfaction, but they'll win at the end. Capricorns have a practical side but sometimes they can be a little excessively. But excessive seriousness could hinder enjoyment, which is something they must be mindful of be. People tend to gravitate towards the Capricorn due to their wisdom and place a high worth on the reliable advice they give. A majority of Capricorns make great companions due to their discretion. They will also remain out of situations they don't believe they have to... regardless of the fact that it's not.

Aquarius - Air Sign

Uranus is the planet of growth, governs Aquarius. The astrology sign of Aquarius has a ability to predict the future with precision and is able to easily adapt to technological advances. Their innovative mind permits them to swiftly ascend to leadership positions. Changes in behavior and policy aren't a problem because they are able to change. The adaptability of Aquarius allows them to be able to embrace the new and exciting things they encounter, and to move with confidence when other people tend to shrink. Aquarius like fantasy and dreaming They are also averse to being influenced by signs that seem too practical may claim that they don't understand the distinction between reality and fiction. But this isn't far from the reality! The Aquarius is well-known by other creative people and those who appreciate Aquarius their sense of humor. Because they are able to judge harshly Aquarius are excellent people to be friends with. In addition they are able to conceal their secrets and connect with those who respect their right to be private.

Pisces Water Sign Sign

The persona of this sign isn't so much focused on the pragmatic or precise aspect of life. It's more interested with the emotional or spiritual side. Pisces may make use of this advantage regardless of the reasons, since the view that this astrological sign provides ensures that they can tackle various challenges in ways that ensure people feel comfortable. A majority of Pisces are artistically inclined. If you are a Pisces profession isn't connected in the field of arts and crafts, they may achieve peace and contentment in a profession that permits them to show their true creative side. In the absence of a suitable venue However, the creative side is evident in everyday life and can be seen in the way their homes are decorated, the way they dress, and in the types of activities they indulge in. A majority of people of this sign will be able to recognize the human emotions It all comes down to Pisces sensitiveness and the ability to see.

Chapter 9: Scorpio 2021 Horoscope: Astro Predictions For The Coming Year

After a long time of nesting, it is time to eventually be able to fly and be able to enjoy the long-awaited recognition! A delicate and sensitive water sign, you'll have the ability to conquer your limitations to showcase your full abilities and abilities to everyone around you. In a non-showering manner, but with a dazzling flair you'll emerge of the forest at the right moment, knowing how to capitalize into an opportunity that isn't expected. An amazing year ahead, filled with personal achievements.

(c) Varvara Gorbash / (c) Varvara Gorbash/123RF

ASTRO SCORPIO 2021

First quarter horoscope 2021

With a fresh look You will be able to bring your ideas to success no matter how original they be. With the effort you've put into it in 2020, you'll be noticed and push your competitors out of the way. Modernity is yours, obsolescence is theirs! With the power of Mars You will be eager to communicate information, demonstrate and convince . Your ability to teach will be acknowledged by your colleagues. As you are rewarded for your achievements, you'll show great confidence. Be careful to ensure that this doesn't become a source of ridicule ...

Horoscopes for the 2nd Quarter of 2021.

Your professional position will be strengthened and you'll lay the foundations for a task which is significant to you. Neptune on your astral realm indicates that your coworkers is trying to limit the extent of your action. You are clearly making him look bad. You might need to be able to behave with more discretion and also to become a better psychologist. If you can learn to anticipate your adversaries, you'll feel more aware of your surroundings. Follow the wisdom of the wise Capricorn .

Horoscope for the 3rd Quarter of 2021.

Field of movement and spiritual growth House IX will keep you away from your comfort zone. The beginning of summer will appear to coincide with an important trip for the rest of your professional career . Expatry is likely to be the order of the day. Moving to a new location, changing language, climate You will be euphoric in the prospect of jumping in the dark. The long-term presence of Mars within your astral horizon makes you completely blind to any kind of argument. Your quest to be absolute and your desire to succeed will not allow up in the face of challenges.

Fourth quarter 2021 horoscope

Following the example of King Midas to transform everything you touch into gold even if that means dehumanizing your loved ones to the status of common objects ... The extravagant world that is yours will not leave space for the desires of the heart as well as the displays of affection. The prisoner of your own ivory tower, you'll be able to escape your previous existence, aided in your decision by the many charms of House I, that are akin to the self-image ... The desire for social revenge will strengthen your heart.

Love: What the year promises for Scorpios

The guilt you'll feel for your beloved can make you unrecognizable. In the event that you are either absent or over-invested you'll appear as an omnipresent person. To avoid more complicated explanations, you'll resort to lying (by by omission) which is backed with the 12th House which is home of dissimulation. Single, your horridity of marriage will cause you to smile at the thought of committing publicly . In this case you'll be attracting birds of prey and ready to go home at the first sign of conflict. There's no reason to complain. Love? A hoax.

Horoscope for love for Scorpio The 2021 forecast

The water sign is renowned for its charismatic personality The Scorpio is in love and an unpredictable monarch, capable of bursting into bursts of generosity , as and small punches. He enjoys having the upper hand over his fellow and is not willing to acknowledge his mistakes, out of fear of losing his face. Also, he has a constant anger. The Scorpio may sometimes conquer his demons through showing kindness however, he will sometimes be reminded that there can only be one dominating ... himself.

Money and work in 2021: the forecast for Scorpio

Your work will be undoubtedly your stronghold, your zone of excellence, all through 2021 . Water is a signification of precise mind, sometimes confused in the role of a leader and will not tolerate being faced with the task of proving your strength. But, combining your strengths with the qualities of a sign that is air-based could enable you to gain more influence. If you are financially secure and even successful you could display a staggering greed. Afraid of the reversals of fortune it can be difficult in some situations to rid yourself of a few ill-judged dollars ...

Horoscopes for work for Scorpio What's new for 2021?

Straight from an Racine show, Scorpio loves tragedy. His intense feelings never let him down, and sometimes not in a positive way! He's also a patient person who, more than any other person, knows how to wait his turn. In 2021 the Scorpio will declare its independence, but not after having caused chaos at work! From the rubble this water sign usually is the strength of a Herculean power ...

The horoscope for money for Scorpio What are the most important financial trends for 2021?

A very passionate sign, if there's any, Scorpio can also be a materialistic creature, who is paying attention to his bank accounts in addition to the accounts of other. He is always looking for the best bargain wherever he goes, and is often able to find it due to the fact that the Scorpio is an German Shepherd flair. By 2021 Scorpio is sure to have every possibility of suffering an economic blow. Highly aware of real estate and banking information, he will know how to protect himself with the right people.

Scorpio's health Scorpio this year

The body may show symptoms of weakness in the autumn season . It is possible to experience an occasional seasonal depression, which is treatable by using gentle therapy. In a general sense, you may experience certain ailments that are that are caused by the malfunction in the thyroid. Changes in your eating habits could help. Consuming oysters, seaweed and other foods that are rich in iodine can ease the symptoms and help strengthen your body. Be sure to boost your intake! If you are a little undernourished Your hourglass size will cause concern to the people who are around you.

The family and friendliness of the Scorpio sign in 2021.

A fourth-house, which is in the same way as Cancer is a shield to protect yourself from your own self. A frenzied and erratic child who is enthralled by successes, you'll be swept away by your conscience and, more importantly, by those you love. They will be able to challenge you to face certain facts while reminding you of your obligations and obligations. If you accept the views of your close friends and you're not accepting about those who teach you the "moral lessons" from your peers . 2021 is not going to be without tensions between them.

The Scorpio forecast for 2021 is based on to your ascendant

Ascendant Scorpio Aries

Inspired by Charles Aznavour, you will take pleasure in the old-fashioned pleasures ...

You'll make use of this season to reconnect to the authentic.

Ascendant Scorpio Taurus

Your building instincts will drive your to purchase the stone. However, you'll hesitate between pleasure-buying and rental investment. Your shaky character will cause you to consider purchasing.

Scorpio Ascendant Gemini

There is a chance that you suffer from iron deficiencies that are linked to an anarchic lifestyle. The lunches you eat at the go, as well as your frequent trips to fast food restaurants can have undesirable results. It's time to revamp the food habits of your ancestors.

Ascendant Scorpio Cancer

The heart flutters to the top, you will be revived by the love that you feel upon first glance. Sweet tickets, intimate meetings, subtle allusions, you'll regress back to the innocence of your childhood, and you will be able to touch your heart with a an erupting flame and be amused by the tenderness.

Ascendant Scorpio Leo

Between immaturity and narcissism, you will be a tumbling wreck. If you are used to getting a response every time You will be especially sensitive to anger. The inexplicably sulky mood will reach their peak in the middle of August. Your family members will need to be prepared to not take your feathers.

Ascendant Scorpio Virgo

Your quirky ways could annoy or attract depending on the crowd you are presenting to you. The way you express what is going through your head can be detrimental to you. Be respectful when dealing with strangers.

Scorpio Ascendant Libra

Your privacy can become the best of a friendship you cherish. You're a frequent victim of this character habit to let it not make you think about your own self-worth.

Ascendant Scorpio Sagittarius

Your sense of humor, enhanced due to your influence by Jupiter can help you overcome the melancholy that you're naturally susceptible. The joy of sharing your fears with your family and friends will enable you to not only overcome them, then at least beat them.

Ascendant Scorpio Capricorn

To make yourself more comfortable it is not always easy. You may be willing to betray yourself, and even abandon those that matter to you. But, there is no excuse to hide your beautiful personality.

Ascending Scorpio Aquarius

Your insanity could create the impression that you are being a little bit of a begging! No matter, those whom you want to appeal will be able to see your lack of sophistication to be a bit snobby ...

Ascendant Scorpio Pisces

Your behavior will be modeled to the canine world during your first trimester. Between yelling and gnashing your teeth, you will have a very difficult business!

The mysterious and sensual Scorpion's native Scorpio is beautiful, but not always easy to read when compared to different signs in the Zodiac ... So who can succeed in convincing her to not bite?

COMPATIBILITY FOR SCORPIO-WOMEN

Scorpio woman as well as Aries man

The Ms. Scorpion and Mr. Aries Always ready to go wild they have a turbulent relationship. They are not afraid to fight, but they also are able to appreciate one another. In the event that Aries. Aries manages to prove his loyalty and are able to overcome their disagreements or disagreements, Mrs. Scorpion and Mr. Aries will be able to enjoy their relationship.

Scorpio female and Taurus man

Incredibly mysterious and mysterious, Madame. Scorpion cannot leave Mr. Taurus indifferent. Additionally Ms. Taurus can provide Madame with the qualities she requires because of his altruism and generosity. Together, they'll make an exemplary and deserving couple. The bride. Scorpion must be careful not to injure him, nevertheless, sir, as there will be no second chance.

Scorpio female and Gemini man

The Mr. Gemini knows how to charm the Mrs. Scorpion. He is able to make her feel more sensual However, the game won't be won. Both of them are very critical and negative in their nature and only see their divergences! While Madame is looking for genuineness in the thoughts of her companion, Monsieur will like to lure, wondering whether he'll be able to find a better partner alternative. In the end the relationship could turn detrimental.

Woman from Scorpio and man from Cancer

Mrs. Scorpio's voluminous nature is captivating the Mr. Cancer, who cannot resist her. On the other hand the Mr. Scorpio provides the calm and safety which Mr. Cancer needs. Together, they'll form an enduring relationship where sexuality will become the supreme word.

Scorpio female and Leo man

The Mr. Leo can find his preferred partner within the woman named Mrs.

Scorpio. Gorgeous sensual, she draws attracted attention and is known for showing her side by his side. Together, they'll be in a position to satisfy their sexual cravings. The meeting will occur in the midst of romance however, they must take a few compromises in order for their relationship to shine.

Scorpio woman , and Virgo man

Mrs. Scorpio, delicate and cautious, regrets the lack of trust and calm displayed by Mr. They can reach a consensus when they don't stop from the perception of being too different. After some effort the union can endure if, in peace, each can keep his space.

Scorpio female and Libra man

Their sexuality is what unites them. They complement one another and ensure that their partners are happy. There is only one cloud in their skies is the one of Madame. Scorpion is exclusive and doesn't like the tricks that are played by the Mr. Libra. This is why it will be essential for Mr. Libra to work to find peace in his marriage.

Scorpio female and Scorpio man

A union between Madame as well as Monsieur Scorpio is an endless conflict. They are in love and break each other up. Their respective egos do not help their work. The only observation that needs to be madeis "we need to hope that this doesn't last too long"!

Scorpio woman as well as Sagittarius man

Mr. Sagittarius needs freedom. The woman. Scorpio is possessive but capable of transforming in many ways to maintain her relationship with her partner. Their relationship may be harmonious or spark numerous sparks.

Scorpio female and Capricorn man

Mrs. Scorpio may seem a bit cold at first however, her emotions often are deep. The Mr. Capricorn, sufficiently stable and focused, will know how to calm her. In his company, she'll thrive and enjoy the joy millions of people desire.

Scorpio female and Aquarius man

The Mr. Aquarius is an indisputable thinker. These fantasies enthrall the Ms. Scorpion who would like to return him to the earth. She wants to alter the way she sees it to be more eloquent. It is not a good idea to say that this is a waste of time however beware of disappointments ! !

Top compatibility

Scorpio female and Pisces man

Monsieur. Poisson's gentleness entices his wife Mrs. Scorpion to deploy all her abilities. She will be successful very quickly in getting to know the Mr. Poisson the sexy partner she's always wanted. If she wishes to maintain it, she'll need to reduce the amount of the criticisms she has (such for instance, her lack of energy and power) and learn to appreciate its virtues to their fullest. In their relationship the Mrs. Scorpion will surely have to dress in pants.

COMPATIBILITY FOR MEN'S SCORPIO

Scorpio male and Aries woman

In a relationship of admiration and comparing notes, and adoring one another. Aries and Mr. Scorpion are in a strong and extremely active relationship. Their ferocity unites them, and jealousy is a great addition to their relationships. Mrs. Aries will practice to discover the secrets of the character of her lover and in the event that by nature, the Mrs. Aries and Mr. Scorpion are into competition, their partnership is likely to last.

Man from Scorpio and Taurus woman

The attraction for sexual pleasure of Mrs. Taurus and Mr. Scorpio is evident. The opposite signs are attracted, but their relationship could not be simple. Being both possessive and possessive by nature, they won't give their partners a break! The Mr. Scorpio has a tendency to stay in his own thoughts It's the sole responsibility of the Mrs. Taureau to find the directions.

Scorpio Man and Gemini woman

Mrs. Gemeau is seduced by the charms that is Mr. Scorpion. The resources it plans to use will be enough to lead it to surrender. The Mr. Scorpio is passionate, always seeking equilibrium. His companion, to not to offend him , must be honest, filled with profound feelings and a need for peace. Only when they are at this level that they can achieve their goals.

A man from Scorpio and a woman from Cancer

Their altruism is the basis for their bond. The Mr. Scorpion represents for Mrs. Cancer: strength and the vigor. With a man like this Mrs. Cancer will have the ability show her sexuality and her sensitivity ... shining in her most attractive appearance. With their openness, they'll stay clear of any negative implication and make a wonderful couple. (TOP COMBATIBILITY)

Scorpio Man and Leo woman

Ms. Lion along with Mr. Scorpio are irresistibly attracted to one another. The Mr. Scorpio bewitches her, however Ms. Lion does not like feeling domineering. Their relationship could be golden rivers as well as a tornado. The game's cards are in the hands Mrs. Lion who has to meet her requirements to be in the heart of the Universe.

Man from Scorpio and Virgo woman

The Mr. Scorpio, warm, romantic and possessive, is sure to ensure that his wife. Virgo happy. He'll know how to bring her under his control and soothe her. With her by her side the Mrs. Virgo will be able to thrive, increasing her sexuality and optimism. But, she should be mindful not to allow herself to be consumed by her lover which means losing the self-confidence and autonomy simultaneously.

Man from Scorpio and Libra woman

Monsieur. Scorpio has a lot of attraction. This is the type of man that Ms. Libra is looking for. Together, they'll satisfy the most cravings of their hearts. Ms. Libra could not resist joking about, but she was not the only one. Mister. Scorpion may then see red. Beware !

Scorpio male and Scorpio woman

A union between Madame the Scorpio and Monsieur Scorpio is an endless sequence of discords. They cherish each other but cause each other to fall apart. Their shared egos do not ease their burden. The only comment that can be madeis "we should hope this doesn't last all too long"!

Scorpio male and female

Ms. Sagittarius has undeniable qualities. She is a global thinker and would like to be successful in social settings. Mr. Scorpion understands this but isn't able to stand seeing her go away each when a new problem arises. He'd like to be at centre of everything but isn't likely to achieve getting there. If he is determined to hold the position, he'll have to make it his own responsibility.

Scorpio male and Capricorn woman

Mr. Scorpio's magnetic nature is appealing attracted to the lady. Capricorn. He may appear distant at first However, once he is with her you will see that life is beautiful and enjoyable. They'll be able be a perfect match and will discover how content we can be.

Man from Scorpio and Aquarius woman

Mr. Scorpio may be tempted by the enthralling by Mrs. Aquarius; but their techniques of seduction are entirely different. Mrs. Aquarius is not sensitive to the attraction attracted by the Mr. Scorpio, she would even be inclined to ignore his company. If Mr. Scorpio wants to accomplish his goals then he'll be being forced to limit his passion.

Scorpio Man and Pisces woman

Their encounter will transform their lives. They require affection demonstrations, sensual and sexual relations. Together, they could be able to sign a contract. In addition, they could make an unexpected couple.

Chapter 10: Astroman Scorpio How To Charm Him, Hold Him, But Let Him Go?

The person you've chosen for you was born in the zodiac sign of Scorpio? Be cautious, you may encountered an enthusiast who is averaging 100 miles per hour and trains you alongside him. You will need to be on the same page as him! To charm him (or quit when you're in a position to do so) and not suffer the risk of a fatal bite, adhere to our astrological tips.

(c) 123RF

Do you want to charm an Scorpio man , to keep him or get rid of him? We've got the skills to do it, and we've got twenty years of reading horoscopes that for us to use.

A Scorpio man is extremely passionate. A man who is completely in love. He does not do things on in half (like quiches or love or pout). He is passionate about a job completed, but sometimes it's extremely boring to be so meticulous. However, there is nothing better than a porcine. Also being cute, this Scorpio man is adorable. The Scorpio man has a "perfect" sideis that He doesn't talk about it (alert not to brag unless your ascendant happens to be Leo). In reality, the Scorpio has doubts because he's fragile and requires to be assured. It is better to die rather than admit that. He likes to appear as an individual who has a good handle on his life in a manner that is posy and charming and doesn't require anyone.

When he's in love, he's passionate and serious, looking forward to a romantic story. Even if he is the independent kid (at the beginning) He is a lover of small taste buds and not paying attention to much. Sexually, he's a hot potato. He is thirsty to discover, he wants to steer the ship (he is an perfectionist, not to be forgotten). However, this doesn't stop him from having sexual sex that is full of emotion to appear to float around and he is happy. But , as usual, he barely displays it and reveals it in time.

The three most astro-friendly signs which are compatible to Scorpio : Cancer (very gentle extremely fragile), Pisces (intense sexual relationships), Sagittarius (happy in life).

The zero chance sign : Capricorn, too stubborn, brutal. Tac-tac what. In the event that Scorpio really is interested, then he does not require to be with someone who is more serious than him.

Swaying the Scorpio man

Simple: avoid provoking him as If you think that the Scorpio male has more sweet heart than he appears, he prefers to be in love for a long time. It can be difficult at first to make it impossible to reach, but you can take it one step at a time. A quick message here, a ferocious glance here ... giving the other person your seriousness and generosity. Since that's what he wants from love: balance, stability and reassurance. Also, know that Scorpio is a lover of very sensitive women , and is a part of their lives. Smile brightly and go about with your flag.

Make sure to keep the Scorpio man

As time passes, the story opens. If you're patient and the story could devour the wall in just three minutes. In other words, we can keep an Scorpio by being honest and honest. Because as a Scorpio cannot lie and he is very involved when he is loved (it can make you cry) and also requires love, just as did his former best friend Lorie (a Taurus ascendant Pisces and the Pisces has a strong affinity to Scorpio). Also, that's the reason Scorpio is quite obsessive. We should also remember that Scorpio enjoys humor, funny jokes and cheerful people. Let's suppose that it does him well, especially if he gets irritated when he does not have his mayo. Therefore, we try to maintain the Scorpio man in check by telling himthat Your mayonnaise is great.

Do not be afraid to love an Scorpio

Scorpio is a person who likes the top , but don't be afraid to enjoy having the bottom. Also, the Scorpio is also a lover of very sexual relationships, regardless of appearances. Feelings, emotions, sweetness ... let it go and kiss Garou.

The Scorpio man

Be kind, he's still extremely sensitive. Make sure you do it correctly since a job that's not completed can cause him to become insane. Therefore, avoid sending it via sending an SMS that is misspelled (especially in the event that you wish to retrieve it someday). Be sure to be cautious by telling your friend "it's not you but me" (since the Scorpio needs to be assured). Before you go you must be aware you are in the Scorpio sign. Scorpio is extremely attentive to the comments that could be made to him , and that he is always looking to outdo himself to ensure the happiness of his companions (when they love him and wants to know whether he is in love with you too). It is never too early to talk to him about your concerns that you may have since he's sure to be able to look after himself. It's not always given to any sign So take a moment to think about it.

The testimonies that make a difference: " I breadcrumbed a Scorpio and he lost confidence in himself so that he phoned his ex-girlfriend back. Today, I'd like to return however, it appears that she's so flawless that they are both in a state of orgasm. "

Chapter 11: What Is Your Preferred Sexual Activity Based On Your Signification Astrological

Each horoscope sign has its own way of sexualizing! It all depends upon whether you're Aquarius, Gemini or Virgo... The first are more into role-playing games, while the other threesomes, and the third one, sadomasochism. The sex horoscope offers numerous ideas to fulfill your desires. Nothing is better than spice up your marriage!

If you've ever dreamed of having a sexual encounter on a boat it's not unusual, you're Pisces! Aries are the more ardent followers of the naturism. Since the astrological sign you are born under can influence your sexual life !

Each sign of the astrological zodiac has its own rituals for sexuality

Aquarius: Role play

You don't care about what people consider and you're enjoying living life to the max. You're not afraid to experiment with new ideas .

Do you want to try the role playing game ? With your partner , pretend to be complete strangers.

Apart from enthralling you, this dream also expands your imagination. How long do you have to stay engaged in the game? It's your choice to choose.

Fish: Making Love on an inflatable boat

Titanic is leaving its footprint! There's nothing to be surprised about since you're a water sign . Instinctively You let yourself be swept in the sea. As time passes you begin to imagine.

Are you two adventurers eager to find a desert island? Two bird-watchers who found the love of their lives on an adventure within the Galapagos? Two passengers of first class who are looking forward to the Captain's dinner? On the boat you can have any fantasies .

Aries Nudist holidays for adult travelers

Nothing is shocking now and you're confident enough in your body for a relaxing adult nudist getaway .

A few people can be intimidating You are able to easily begin discussions with your fellow couples. Furthermore, you're quite proud of your appearance as well as that of your spouse. Therefore, why not share it with everyoneelse?

Cancer The body is painted with paint

What's better than trying out new things with your loved one, all as you make artwork? Let him scribble across your body using his hands stuffed with paint. Together, you create an artwork and your sensitive side adores it!

Virgo: Being domineering

You've always felt that you were a hot dominatrix . Your partner will be able to see that hidden part of you can drive them mad.

He's wait for your to decide to take the matter in your own hands. You're feeling free. You no longer have to fear the gaze of other people because you were created to be an effective leader.

Libra Testing Orgasmic Meditation

You love the fact that things are taking time and get very intense. This is the perfect meditation for you!

This kind of yoga lets you focus on the pleasure shared by both partners. An hour-long session is the ideal time to feel a genuine sexual intimacy for two .

Sagittarius Replay sex scenes from your most cherished films

You don't think too much about yourself and aren't afraid of ridicule. You can spend the entire weekend reliving sex scenes from your favourite movies.

What is it? The 50 Shades torture room , Ghost's blow to the pottery or frolics in the field of wheat as the one in Match Point?

Before you begin, make the following list of your most memorable scenes. The laughter, the giggles, and the fun are is guaranteed!

Capricorn: Eating foods while on the body of another

For you gourmets! Go to the refrigerator and take out the strawberry liquid chocolate, the whipping cream ...

All you need to do is put these sweets on body parts you want to treat. Suck, swallow, or lick ... the choice is all up to you!

What is the most astrological symbol is appropriate for threesomes?

Gemini: Have an impromptu Threesome along with your companion

The threesome was designed to please you, dear Gemini! If you are bored easily You will not get bored by the countless options offered by this method of sexuality. Be observant, take part, switch partners, the choice is yours.

Leo is the perfect patch for a trio

A lot of couples are searching for the ideal partner for threesome . You're the one ! Be prepared to be lavishly treated in the way it ought to be. In fact, without you, this trio would not even exist.

Enjoy yourself and show off your skills. This isn't the moment to resign, as your audience is in your presence!

Taurus: Watching couples are having sex at a night

There is no one who is aware of this, but you are an observer. Instead of slapping your head first, you like to look around.

For more information take a trip to an sex-themed party together with your companion. Make a promise to watch only at the time you arrive.

The resistance will turn you on even more , and you'll be able reproduce the same thing you saw at home. The next time, you'll attend the fun.

Scorpio: Take in the role of your companion

Since a long time you've wanted to change the roles . You've been through your domineering stage, even before the huge triumph with the 50 Shades of Gray.

You'll be enthralled by playing roles with your man. To accomplish this, grab the strap-on dildo, and then try to test the penetration!

All you have to do is jump in!

Chapter 12: What Zodiac Sign Are You The Most Sexually Compatible With?

It's true, sexual compatibility could also be based on your zodiac sign! In reality, sexual attraction isn't only an issue that you are physically attracted. It's about having a spiritual connection to your companion. Certain signs work together more than others. For instance, do you have Aries Taurus Or Cancer? This is the perfect time to discover which of the astrological signs you have the most chemistry sexually with!

Astrological signs that have the most sexual chemical chemistry

Aries and Libra compatibility: a couple working for each other

In the world of life, and especially in love, when Aries desires something, he can't do it four directions.

Contrary to Libra who is a thinker, Libra will think through both the advantages and disadvantages before making a choice.

She's best suited to emulate the fiery spirit of Aries to a degree. Aries, with his determination and unwavering optimism, is able to calm Libra.

Together, they make up an untypical couple , but one that is successful. They are curious about each other and they love one another a lot.

When they're in bed, they're extremely attentive to the needs of their partner and are determined to bring their dreams reality .

The compatibility Gemini and Sagittarius is a couple who's not afraid of anything

Gemini as well as Sagittarius make the greatest energetic pair ever! It's simple, they're unafraid of anything.

Being in love outdoors by using sextoys or sex toys, and being a trio... it's no problem! The more exciting and adventurous the idea is, the more they'll desire to make it happen.

The two signposts are thrilled to have found in each other one a partner in gaming who is willing to play with all the tricks.

Taurus and Scorpio compatibility: a couple of epicureans

When they are in romance, Taurus and Scorpio have all their senses alert. Together, they make some of the most romantic duets.

The desire that Scorpios for intimacy is perfectly blended with the sexual desires of Taurus. The two have a tough to leave the room when they are.

Their romance is so sensual that it appears to be straight from a film.

Which astrological sign should you choose to sexual relations with?

Cancer and Capricorn compatibility: when opposites are attracted

Nobody embodies this phrase more than these two indications. Cancerians are imaginative, flirty and fantasies ... different from the serious, focused and common sense Capricorns.

Both are at the opposite side of the spectrum of astrological signs . But their relationship is solid. They both find each other's character intriguing and fascinating.

Their relationship with each other is intense and tense since they must have a romantic exchange with someone completely different. But , in the end, everything is getting resolved.

Leo and Aquarius compatibility : a pair that is full of some spice

People born under the Leo sign are very self-centered and don't appreciate those who try to take over them. They will do anything to have somebody in their bed to satisfy their needs .

Naturally, this leads to difficult situations, particularly for their loved ones such as a one-sided relationship, love displeasure , broken heart ...

The Aquarians are the only people that can bring them back to their proper place. They are admired for their intelligence as well as their detachedness.

They are awe-inspiring to Leo and they begin to realize that they're not in control. They're even beginning to enjoy it.

In the bed, Aquarians always have unexpected ideasthat Leo can easily satisfy.

A good match Virgo and Pisces is the most surprising couple

Virgos are distant, practical and logical. They are grounded. Pisces On contrary, are in a fairytale and can be a bit upside down.

Chapter 13: The Main Story For The Year

2021 is going to be an year of reflection on your life. You can step into the spotlight the darkest moments, to discover what's happening in your heart

What is important to the Scorpio is the fact that you're an individual who is not ruined by anyone else. The only one who is able to make you feel go down or up is yourself and that is why you must find your heart. It's a factor that can lead you to a beautiful way.

This year this year, you'll be living in an increasingly personal life. They will isolate themselves from the world around them more despite physical interaction with a lot of people, your mind will be separated. You'll be able to cover yourself, and secretly. In the bustle of life like at home, you will not worry much about what's going on around you. Don't bother about the about the world, don't bother with the media, but if you do be anything, they'll be more willing to indulge me, yet in the same way you won't look more powerful.

Or change the persona In the event that they do, then people will think you are the same. Some people may look soft, soft, not even dangerous. But you're different.

Another intriguing story This year, you'll be able pay more focus on the forces that are around you. Perhaps you're attracted by the magic of the universe, mysterious power of the universe, the cosmic dimensions, or even the awe-inspiring. It makes you want to connect with things that are difficult to define. If you're interested in learning to meditate using divination cards and practicing magic spells Find the perfect instructor.

Chapter 14: Finance And Money

It is your goal to do better this year. It was an amazing year to save gold. Life planning for the long term, which includes different types of investments and purchasing insurance to provide the future.

What's important to you? This will also help you earn more money and yield fruits, and you might begin investing in different forms. Since borrowing personal loans You can to be a part of the company of your friends or purchase real estate for this year. Still outstanding in purchasing spoons, home, or leaving mortgage second-hand items to earn profits and the goal to create projects that can be paid in full later.

If you're a liabilist or have a tight budget, you hand, then you will need to find someone to help you and should you have inheritance requirements such as a car, an apartment or invest for improvements to your home. You will bring the joy that meets the expense.

The Job

This year's forecast warns of chaos that comes from working with the mass of people. Conflicts that occur every day. There will be conflict periodically and there'll be an atmosphere of tension. I seldom have a good relationship with my colleagues.

If you are employed within a firm or an organization that is connected to a large number of people who work together In the event that your heart gets exhausted, it is common to fall into the minority. No one listens to your voice. And vice versa, you have to be careful to keep separated. To avoid having to be involved in the midst of.

Work-life in the coming year will go at a slow pace in the corporate office there's going to be chaos. There are a lot of people who are working in and out. There are issues on all levels. If you run the business yourself, you'll often face problems from your employees, which is not which is the most enjoyable work. So, it is usually done on your own. There's no need to be with anyone.

The Lover

There will be more opportunities to let your heart open. or have created a different mood in your relationship.

However long they've been in a relationship, It will be the same there are many lessons that must be taken into consideration. This year there will be a set of criteria to take a vacation with someone you're acquainted with. There are important traveling dates. It is possible to deepen your relationship. If you aren't sure if you want to be loved and getting released with your friends, there are things to be aware of in the coming year. If you meet someone, the mind will be completely captivated. It is possible that you won't be able hear the other person's voice. I would like to encourage you to step back to keep a relationship that isn't too uncomfortable.

12 Months

January:

It's casual work and an opportunity may appear to him, but if he's quick and hasty, then certain criteria may fail to be met by business owners, executives, and employees are cautious, employees could create problems with the money and the first month is still in good state to make use of however, the entire month is cautious to not make losses on cars and communication equipment. When traveling, it might encounter obstacles that slow down or cause issues with your companion.

February

It isn't necessary to travel far , whether it's an educational seminar or a neighborhood.

It's well-positioned to help singles meet someone who can make you feel happy and eliminate loneliness within only a few months but it's still in a constant state which should be taken care of by employees. Employees who cause problems with lobbying Avoid doing so in a hurry , which does not benefit your health which should be taken care of. be more careful, however the money is important. Be extra cautious because there is a requirement to be able to search someone else to travel with, or

March

could be a source of conflict with lovers and spouses that need patience to ensure their marriage and relationships with singles, friends and family members. There is a chance that I will be in love and find an ideal partner in a private career or full-time job There is the possibility that it will succeed. If there is someone else in the relationship, you should be aware of finances, as it could create problems with finances if you're decorating, fixing housesor homes. Be cautious, as the expenses will increase.

April

succinct. Don't hesitate to ask for help, particularly when dealing with agents, trading, brokers or job-seekers. However, if you're the owner of the company and management, you should not overestimate the work of the employees. It could cause harm to important work of money. You must be cautious about all relationships, specifically with the opposite gender. Additionally, you could lose money. Still can argue until it is damaged.

May

The business of brokerage is a good one. They have to put in a lot of effort and compete, and fight hard for more opportunities, but if one isn't careful regarding the signing of contract documents could put them in a disadvantage. In the case of relationships, singles who work might find romance and find their soul mate However, with a romantic relationship that is at the end of the bucket, it must be put at risk. If convicted, they will have to be a hard-working person to stand a an opportunity to win.

June

Finances are included in the requirements. In either the case of the partner or partner, the contractual party or any other parties that should be extra cautious when intending to sign a contract or contract for any type of commercial work, regular work is going to be a smooth distance that doesn't need to work hard. But If you decide to resign, applying for another job ... extremely risky! If you are in love, and you're on the "giving" side do not say it, do not be angry if someone decides to spend more money. Are they in good health that makes love pleasant.

July

The loss of reputation can be the result of lobbying. Doing business in a dishonest manner! In the field of tourism, foreign relations education, and other fields when it's an ongoing project, it is more likely for success in earning making money from a regular company. It's the primary source of income that can allow you to live more comfortably. Love story Both tourism and travel students are categorized according to their religious beliefs. A common faith can make the love experience enjoyable, and singles are able to meet love and the person they've always wanted to be with.

August

In the best way, if you pay your focus and energy in your venture, it is the best place to start to long-term success. There are more opportunities for with regards to finances, either as a result of a profession or to invest and gamble and cause cash to flow. Love story: Smooth relationships with loved ones love, partners, and lovers are all ready to become ATM cards. Credit cards for singles and friends could be a way to discover the love of their lives. Are you able to meet your love of your life.

September

With finance that is still in the budget to easily use, you could be able to make money without having to run around, but be cautious. Increase profits through "taking any risk" when it comes to rushing and managing work that is not completed. While there's no issue with adults, you must be aware for your subordinates. Employees could create problems and cause trouble. It is not easy to correct. When you're in love, in a harmonious romance, the person is eager to help. Support behind the scenes, but beware of the hidden love which could pose dangers.

October

The earnings are in good shape. However ... you're going to have the cash of the harrowing must be judiciously handled or avoided sharing it with friends who are friends, lovers, or lovers. borrowing because there is a very high risk of creating conflicts and hurting over work, and they must be avoided. "Stab on the back" when you do anything that is in secret, such as slandering other people. Since there is no covert way to go about it anywhere in the world .. making enemies be hurt, there's the chance that it will be a love stories of travel can result in you finding romance and finding your soul mate however, be wary of the person. May bring trouble.

November

Communication that is unclear In addition to keeping in contact Relationships can have issues and can cause conflict. this month, if you need to travel for long distances, don't underestimate the possibility of a situation or risk that can occur unexpectedly regarding money It is important to have a number that is easy to locate and easy to use however, you must be cautious. Cash from being threatened or blackmailed or even from foreigners. I am a huge fan of taking journeys with my loved ones, it's an amazing romantic bond. than a few people get the chance to get to know my soulmate.

December

The month that ends in the last Month of Year, learn how to live is essential. Earn money while spending money in a relaxed manner and using emotion to write, talk, and talk to anyone. Particularly with spouses, lovers or contractors, partners or partners who could be deceiving or arguing, and even breaking up in the course of work. You should take care to only do what's needed. If you postpone, and this month, pay attention to your health, as you could be that you get sick and not feel at ease, also.

Gems/colors that increase prosperityinclude Ruby, Pink gem purple-red.

Gems/colors that are deadly Amethyst in bright purple, amethyst in bright garne

The most beautiful time of week is Tuesday

Lucky Number: 5, 3, 8

The zodiac signification of the fateful acquaintances: Gemini, Leo, Sagittarius, Aquarius

Things to consider being aware about in 2021.

1. To collapse in a difficult situation There are difficulties everywhere. It is difficult to understand the nature of life as a whole.

2. It is the month that is full of chaos. The work you do in this month will be challenging to complete.

3. The month of July can be chaotic. Depression, loneliness and other mental health issues

4. It is August, the month for Nemesis. Bad luck beware of accidents and lawsuits

5. If there's legal disputes that could be a target We will have to confront a serious injustice.

6. Engage in the war. It's like being compelled to be the leader on the battlefield.

7. Sculpting joyful faces.

8. Numerology 5 and number 8 usually bring bad luck. You should be cautious in your application of the numbers 5 and 8.

9. Beware of fraudsters who make money even though you put in a lot of money in your final days.

10. Hormone fluctuations. The impact on physical and mental health. Depression but do not want to visit an doc.

10 creative ways to present yourself in 2021

1. What do you receive Are all good enough? The important thing is to ensure that others are not smacking your head. Don't take your head of the person who is slapping it.

2. Sensitiveness or could it be referred to Sense Hunch? Sometimes, it will reveal a secret.

3. Money belongs to the outside world. However, it can be used to purchase happiness.

4. Do whatever you want to be able to pay for it as a base. In the beginning you shouldn't be able to refuse the need to earn money.

5. It is important to have an idea. However, keeping it going is expensive. If you are able to keep the streak going. You'll earn amazing rewards following

6. The best month to be in is July.

7. The month of July also has significant pins. The events that take place in July will have a significant impact on your daily life.

8. Even if you aren't connected to anyone, but you are you in need of meeting new people , beware of being lost in a place that's getting becoming darker each day.

9. Sometimes, you have to get out of difficulties. It takes courage at first.

10. The state of mind. The opposite could be a point of entry for opening new areas for greater understanding.

Chapter 15: Scorpio Love Match

Marriage Profile

A happy marriage will likely to be one where your spouse is gentle and yielding to your full instructions. You are very proud of your personal qualities and the things you have to offer which is why you expect a huge amount from every partnership. In any relationship, you don't ever completely surrender all that you can offer however, you usually have plenty to give. Your nature is to be loyal to your spouse, however you're not content to just sit in your home and watch the world go through. You will never want to end your union once the true love has been shown and you strive to make improvements to everything that is not harmonious in the relationship. The Scorpio husband is a tyrant, jealous and demanding. The Scorpio wife can leave her family members in a state that is characterized by nervous exhaustion due to her erratic anger.

The Marriage Partner

It is said that the Scorpio husband is among the most difficult people to be with peaceful and harmonious. This is possible when his wife is open to his ideas and adheres to what he says. He can be difficult to ignore when the tenacity of his thoughts is evident in everything that he would like to do. He is certain that he is the household's head and is determined to be recognized as the head of the household. Sometimes, he takes this attitude to the extreme, and a divorce is inevitable. There are greater chances of happiness for a moderate Scorpio spouse, who is typically prosperous and able to provide for a wife and a an extended family. But, his overt commitment and obsession with his wife can cause an issue for his family. However much attention and affection he gets He is usually insecure and unsure and will alter things in his head in order to make them appear to be against him. It's all in his mind, however he is still angry and frustrated.

The wife of the Scorpio loves marriage and all of its responsibilities extremely seriously and holds a traditional respect for the domestic duties. If her behavior changes and she loses her sense of love, she'll follow whatever her heart dictates and often without the fear of consequences. She's not fooled, and doesn't believe in illusions neither does she attempt to trick herself, but she accepts reality in a straightforward and rational way. The Scorpion husband has a genuine and deep love for his wife and children, yet the Scorpio husband can be extremely unselfish and stubborn. The wife of a Scorpio invests her whole heart in her devotion to her husband and her family however, she doesn't take her family members for granted. Because she views life a bit too realistically, she perceives the people she loves as they truly are.

Children

You would like to have an extended family, even when you might fall in the sphere of parental responsibility. You could be a harsh parent, even if you have great intentions, but in the end, these are worth it. Your temperament could be unsuitable since you may be domineering, possessive or even violent. Yet, you nearly always get married and have a lot of children. The children of Scorpio have intense feelings of affection and care must be taken when developing them so that they do not get damaged by excessive indulgence on one hand and harshness to the contrary. While they're physically robust, their emotional character requires the highest care. Parents often feel that they are difficult to deal with, and they can become problematic youngsters when not understood. Selfishness and insecurity are typical errors that parents need to attempt to correct.

Home

Even though you're not suited to a well-ordered home, you're capable of adapting, and when you're settled, you can apply all the control and energy of your enthusiastic nature to your house. You are gifted at creating an environment that is relaxing, and even lavish. Your home is usually tastefully built, but it may also seem more lavish than modest. You're very proud of your family and friends and would like to showcase them in a space you believe they deserve. It gives you an outlet for your creative and artistic impulse, which is quite robust. Sometimes, the wild side of your personality can get out of hand. You are the ultimate boss at home, and you're always looking for to have the final say in every issue. This is due to the belief that there is no other choice just as good as yours. The environment can play an important aspect in your success. the warmth and trust found at home are essential.

Chapter 16: Scorpio Cusps

About Cusps

What is it that it means being born at the cusp?

Western Astrology is based upon the Sun. As it is the case that Western calendar is solarand that is based on the motions of the Sun and the Sun, so too it is also the Western Zodiac. This is different from Eastern astrology , which relies on lunar (moon) and based on moon. Each astrological system give insight into a person's personality, their life, and the potential future. Solar astrology is based on the path of the Sun through the sky all year. The birth sign of a person is determined by the area of sky in which the Sun stood in the moment of their birth. The motion in the orbit of Earth's Earth within the Sun results in that the Sun seem to move through the sky. The path is represented by the symbols that make up the Zodiac and is split into twelve sections with thirty degrees each. The term Zodiac originates in the Greek word "zoon" which means living thing, as the majority of the constellations that are in the Sun's path are depicted by animals. Each constellation is a part or section in the sun's path. Each of these sections measures thirty degrees wide and the Sun changes from one to the next one as the year passes through.

However, that change is not immediate. Since it appears that the Sun appears to move due to the Earth's rotation it slowly moves between signs and to the following. This implies that the traits of any sign may change based on when an individual is born. Additionally, certain people are born near the cusp. This is the line that divides the thirty-degree segment and another. The characteristics conferred by a specific sign are not absolute, and astrologers have to be aware of this when making charts. We will explore the characteristics of being born on the threshold between signs and what traits are evident but are fading, and what traits are in the present and growing based on the Zodiac sign the Sun is moving between.

Libra Scorpio Cusp

This is a shift that makes a great investigator, the police force or private. Libra is intelligent, smart and has a keen perception of the law. Scorpio is tough and determined but not too stubborn. It also has a keen sense of emotional responses from other people. Scorpio is able to be almost sensitive at times. The combination of intellect and emotional intelligence makes Libra-Scorpio a powerful character who is difficult to deceive.

Scorpio is among those rare signs that are controlled by two planets in this instance Mars as well as Pluto. Mars can bring aggression as well as an attitude of entitlement. Scorpios believe that they are entitled to the positive things that happen to them, and they're not unwilling to say so. Pluto divinity of the dark side is a dark element that is expressed in different ways depending on the place the place of birth at the time of the change. People born near Libra will display a more calculating mind. The Libran sense of justice is diminished as the Scorpio affected Libra is determined to tilt the balance towards their favor. The people born close to

Scorpio will be afflicted with very strong emotions and will leave emotional scars that are hidden.

Libra represents the 7th signification that is part of the Zodiac and Scorpio is the eighth. Libra is quite intellectual. However, as Libra moves into Scorpio there is less interest in academic pursuits, and more attraction to emotional activities, like dating or playing any sport that provides an emotional thrill.

Each Libra and Scorpio are incredibly loyal companions and can want the same degree of loyalty from each other. The Scorpio-Libra cusp will be treated with respect and their companion will be more concerned about having a peaceful and peaceful home than an outgoing Libra will be. Although Libra isn't a party animal as Taurus, Libra does enjoy the company of intelligent people and is a fan to pursue intellectual interests. Scorpio is not as concerned with the mind and more interested in the heart. This combination will be balanced around mid-point. Libra is more likely to have a relaxed attitude, while Scorpio is a lover of conversations and reading. This cusp is most effective when it is paired with one who is at least an intellectually equivalent. Gemini as well as Aquarius represent two zodiac signs which match the Libra-Scorpio cusp perfectly.

The Libra-Scorpio human is an excellent communicator and adept at conceptual thinking These are two traits learned from Libra. From Scorpio is a deep interest in people as well as a desire for stability and family life. The Libra-Scorpio cusp fascinated by you and to take a great interest in children, particularly their own. The Libra phase of this transformation will pull Scorpio away from emotions. However, the Scorpion has strong emotions, that's why this results having emotions a bit more suppressed than they normally are. The water signs Scorpio is secretive like all water signs. the air sign Libra isn't in a position to alter this characteristic in any way. This could cause problems when Scorpio has a secret requirement that he doesn't reveal, but wants you to be aware of the issue anyway.

These two signs possess plenty of intelligence and depth. When you combine them, you'll get quite a mix. A Libra-Scorpio cusp can be described as a person who is extremely committed, deeply loved, is able to keep secrets in good order and is a bit risky. If you are a fan of thing.

Scorpio Sagittarius Cusp

Its symbolism for Scorpio can be described as The Scorpion while The Archer symbolizes of Sagittarius. Scorpio is a water sign , while Sagittarius is the fire sign. Scorpio is an unchangeable sign meaning that the traits that a person was born with are seldom changed over the course of their lives. This is quite different from other mutable signs, such as Gemini, Aquarius and yes, Sagittarius. It's not always a bad thing. Fixed signs can be more durable. They possess a stick their nature, which isn't found in the mutable signs. They aren't willing to quit or abandon any activity after they've committed their minds to it. This characteristic tends to alter Sagittarius's less persistent traits. This is in many aspects beneficial. Sagittarius is excellent for identifying targets but it isn't always adept in hitting them. Its presence Scorpio within the cusp makes the archer's target more precise.

The Scorpio-Sagittarius shift is often known as "the Cusp of Revolution. The people born in this time typically have issues with authority and tend to do what they would like to do regardless of the disapproval or approval of their peers. This is an individual and impulsive cusp, which can be difficult to be around especially when you're the one giving the directives. Scorpio-Sagittarius individuals expect those in power to have earned the position by being correct most of the time, rather than being wrong. A cusp person is prone to judging any authority, no matter if the authority is happy with it or not.

A wild , youthful person is typically the signification of the Scorpio-Sagittarius cusp. This transition is unique in its features and does not fit well with other. This could make a Scorpio-Sagittarius person feel unique and could make them feel like they're not a part of the group. Yet, they typically feel a conviction. But, this goal might not be the typical way to pursue an occupation. The deep emotions of Scorpio blends with the pure motives of Sagittarius to produce a person who is more interested in doing right instead of making a profit. This is a mystical sign that may struggle with in becoming practical and objective.

www.ingramcontent.com/pod-product-compliance
Lightning Source LLC
Chambersburg PA
CBHW050408120526
44590CB00015B/1886